Paths Are Made by Walking

A Step-by-Step Guidebook
for Spiritual Self-Discovery

Rosalind Thompson, M.A., MFCC
with MaryAnn Gutoff

Paths Are Made by Walking

copyright ©1997 by Rosalind Thompson

Printed in the United States of America

ISBN 0-9657600-0-6

Dedication

My endless gratitude and love to Marie Smith, my teacher and friend, who always sees the highest in me, teaches me to trust the process and celebrates my growth.

Acknowledgements

To MaryAnn Gutoff, with whom I share a special bond, my gratitude for her skills as an editor, organizer of thoughts, questioner, believer.

Special thanks to Margot Silk Forrest, who lent her wordsmithing and her heart to this project, and to Barbara Rose Billings, who gave support and encouragement in the process.

Thanks also to Nancy Evans, who moved naturally into the role of birth coach for this book, making the details easier to manage. My gratitude and admiration to Elena Fiant, who rises above circumstance to express spirituality.

Thank you to countless clients, who taught me to search deeper within for answers.

There are no accidents! I am grateful that all our paths merged and that this guidebook is a result. May you all know how special you are, and may you all know peace.

Forward

My foundations for understanding human behavior rests on my graduate degree in counseling and on serving as a licensed marriage and family counselor since 1980. Spiritual studies opened my eyes and my heart, completing the puzzle.

Once I had experienced enough spiritual growth to look at life differently myself, I asked the Universe for a way to share this process with others. The answer to my request is the content of this book.

This book is not about me, though I peek out from time to time. It presents a framework for understanding life and how spiritual development can either be blocked or nurtured. I am not here to intercede with the Divine for you. You must do your own work your own way.

I show you the path I still walk as a student. I show you how to love and heal yourself.

Contents

1

Getting Started

Why walk in the dark when you can have the presence of the Light?

The 1990's is soul time. Angels, meditation tapes, yoga classes and books on spirituality are everywhere. More and more spiritual seekers are turning to non-traditional practices. Some who were raised in established western religions are finding them too restrictive, too centered on a leader who intercedes for them with the Divine. They long to connect with God in a personal way.

As the millennium approaches, people are seriously trying to understand and express peace on earth, forgiveness, love, and living their own truth on a daily basis. For many of us, these are words that we understand but find increasingly difficult to express in our lives in the face of intensifying societal and personal problems, the aging of relatives and our time being overfilled with obligations.

People want to feel competent at being spiritual and their souls long for connection with the Divine. But when forgiveness is too difficult, or there is no peace in the heart, or loving seems to draw more pain, we feel like failures. Some people respond by seeking different routes to spiritual study while others shut down and declare that God is dead.

As I explored spirituality and psychology from many angles and with many teachers over a lifetime, I always felt inept. Missing from many studies of spirituality, religion and psychology are instructions for how to forgive, love and be at peace. I didn't know how to get past anger, resentment, guilt and shame. I pointed my anger at others for their lack of love and peacefulness. I even moved away from God for nearly 20 years. It took a personal crisis for me to reconnect. Over time though, God has become my first resource rather than my last resort.

Once I became aware of the "how to" of arriving at a peaceful state and living in the flow of Divine guidance, I simply had to write this book. My joy and my responsibility is to teach others how to feel successful as spiritual beings.

This book reflects my life and my studies of both psychology and spirituality. In it, you will find the connection between your psyche and your soul. You will be encouraged over and over to do it your way, at your pace, because this is your journey. Personal growth and spiritual development are one and the same. Using your own inner wisdom, you will be shown how to move from knowledge to healing. You will learn to erase the fear that keeps you alone.

This is a do-it-yourself book for the soul, a practical, step-by-step guidebook to spiritual self-discovery. Let us begin...

Honoring Yourself

You are a growing evolving being, a distinct individual soul on this earth — here to learn whatever it takes to refine yourself and grow closer to the Divine. I encourage you to celebrate your truth, to honor and act from your unique perspective. When you recognize how different you really are from every other soul, you can appreciate how important it is for you to create your own spiritual path. No other soul can or should do it just the way you do. You will come to know every aspect of yourself in order to learn your particular soul refinement lessons. This is the reason for your journey, your life.

Throughout this guidebook, I encourage you to take personal responsibility for every moment of your life, for each decision, reaction, thought, word and deed because personal growth enhances spiritual growth. I will describe at length how to go about taking responsibility, why it is essential and how it ultimately leads to freedom.

The spiritual journey is a personal journey, but it is at the same time intrapersonal — between God and us, and interpersonal — between other people and us. We need God because we are all His children and our souls long to return to Him. We need other people to bring our life lessons, and to provide guidance and support along the way.

Benefits Of Spiritual Work

Why would you work at self-understanding and spiritual growth if you suspect you'll unearth emotional discomfort in the process? Because spiritual understanding offers hope and the knowledge that there is a Divine plan for you. Because you realize you're trapped in a repetitive loop that no longer feels right and you've realized you have the courage to seek change. And, because your soul demands it. Once you've committed to your personal process, you'll know that whatever happens in your life is for your growth. Continuing, conscious spiritual growth will allow you to feel freer and stronger by helping you to:

◊ Avoid repetitive mistakes

◊ Live more simply

◊ Have abundant energy

◊ Feel youthful

◊ Be free of internal pressure to perform

◊ Know who you are

◊ Be unafraid

Getting Started

Imagine a straight line extending into infinity. That is The Way. All religions believe that there is a defined code of behavior and thought leading directly to Paradise, Nirvana, the dwelling place of the Divine. The Bible speaks of it as going "through the eye of the needle." It is that narrow a set of rules — no margin for error. I know that God (or whatever name you choose to call The Source of us all) is much bigger than that, much more forgiving. God is capable only of unconditional love. Therefore, our steps off "The Way" are designed to create lessons, which are reminders that we need to notice our decisions, reactions and choices. Staying closer to The Way makes living easier but can't be accomplished until each person understands and makes this choice for himself or herself. We learn about The way and make these choices on what is often called the "spiritual path."

Unlike The Way, your path — your spiritual journey — twists and turns. Sometimes many other paths cross it, other times only a few, and now and again, you walk alone. Others cross your path both to teach you and to be taught. When you learn to see what they are really teaching, you move beyond the limitations of your mind and begin to see and understand with a higher wisdom. I call this seeing with your heart.

Thus you begin, consciously putting one foot in front of the other on your spiritual path, keeping yourself open to new ways of thinking, feeling and behaving as your life teaches you how to refine your soul. As you open further, you will also discover how to be of service to others and how to return home to the Divine.

Today is a good day to start taking responsibility for your spiritual journey. Listen to your heart. Is it urging you to begin? If, at first, you feel fear, just realize that fear is a product of the mind, not the heart. Most people resist change. The first step toward a conscious life is always the hardest. But if you genuinely believe the time is not right for you to open to spiritual growth, then wait. Whether you choose to start your journey today, or in decades to come, your soul's path back home to the Divine will wait. This is no small commitment. Once you open yourself to a new consciousness, you will be provided with all you need to develop further. One step leads to the next, the next and the next. Your steps actually create the path. It forms under your feet as you walk it. *Paths are made by walking!*

As you think about the magnitude of your decision to embark on a conscious spiritual journey, you may realize that it calls for an entirely new way of living. It does — but why not create a new way? Has the old way made you feel centered and strong? If not, be assured that when you consciously walk your own path, you will come to know your own power. Let others do what they will. This decision is yours alone. No one can make it for you and you can make it for no one else. To progress on your own path, you cannot expect others to think, feel, behave or perceive as you do. Your spiritual path is all about coming to know yourself, your way, as unique as your experiences have made you.

I have been studying and pursuing my own spiritual growth for years. Increasing awareness has lighted my way through some very dark times. As I move through my own process, I have come to understand the roles I play in my life, so that everyday living becomes easier and smoother, less fraught with emotions like helplessness and despair.

Finding and maintaining inner peace are the goals that drove me to seek a spiritual path. (I still receive daily lessons on that subject!) I began my awakening by studying life experiences and my reactions to them. As I evolve, I discover how tremendously nurturing and complete life can be when I live it consciously. Sharing my developing knowledge with my clients has been a natural outgrowth of my process, and this guidebook serves to speak to an even wider audience. In the chapters to come, I will discuss spiritual concepts in practical terms. My intent is to support you in taking responsibility for your spiritual journey. The concepts and lessons within this book help you to create your own "safe container," within which you can explore who you really are. This book will help you — step by step — to expand your container as needed, so that you can hold and accept what you find. Seeing what's there is more than half the battle.

Peace comes from flowing with your life experiences.

⊗ Tools

Along the way, through study, guidance and meditation, I have discovered a number of tools to help me stay focused and balanced despite external events and internal turmoil. Any repair job goes easier when you have the right tool. There's a different one for each kind of project. The tool is a device you pull out and use as needed. On the spiritual path, you are your own repair worker. When you carry a box of tools, you are ready for whatever you find.

Spiritual tools are portable. They are all words filled with love.

I'll share these tools with you in the pages that follow. I offer them as concepts about how life works, as reminders to you, but not as specific rules. Since this guidebook encourages you to find your own way, you will need to adapt these tools to your own perspective and life circumstances. When you see this mark ⊗ at the beginning of a sentence, a tool follows.

Here's your first spiritual tool. ⊗ *Your steps actually create your spiritual path.* It forms under your feet as you walk it! Therefore, if you don't like the direction your life is headed, move your feet in a new direction.

Building Blocks for Spiritual Growth

In this book I will present the steps of the spiritual journey in a sequence that will guide you along your path. These steps build upon one another much as a house is built on its foundation. Commitment is the foundation of your spiritual house. Without commitment, your sense of spirituality feels shaky and uncertain. Once you realize that spiritual development is a long-term process, you'll avoid a great deal of the temptation to compare yourself and compete with where other people seem to be on their paths. Your commitment becomes spiritual self-discovery.

Rising from the foundation of commitment are the four walls of compassion, willingness, patience and faith. I will discuss each of these concepts in concrete terms, rather than as lofty, unattainable ideals. I will also describe common human traits that interfere with the construction of your walls (and with inner peace). They include anger, judgment, fear and guilt. Once you recognize and understand these traits within yourself, you can remove them, but not without exercising compassion, willingness, patience and faith. In addition, we'll explore forgiveness, with an emphasis on not rushing into it before you are ready.

The roof of your spiritual house is understanding the role of guidance in the process of spiritual growth. In the chapter on refinement, you'll explore your house's interior design. Its exterior will emerge in being of service. Finally, the chapter on following your own path will create the landscaping. The house isn't complete until all the elements are in place. You are its designer and builder. God gives you the materials. You do the work, one step at a time.

About The Terminology

I designed *Paths Are Made by Walking* to embrace all religions, spiritual practices and ways of thinking. This open approach creates a challenge in regard to which words to use. To keep my meaning as clear as possible, I offer the following glossary of terms. Feel free to discard any term that doesn't fit for you and replace it with your own word. This is your journey. Make this book yours, too.

Glossary

God	Higher Power, Universe, Divine, Light, Holy Spirit, Goddess, Source
The way	The quickest route Home, the Christ life
Path	The route you are taking, your life
Heart	Inner knowing, higher self
Mind, Outer Mind	Ego, fear, thoughts in reaction to external events
Heal	Learn from what hurts or is unfinished in order to reduce automatic negative emotional responses, to become peaceful (Notice that "heal" is very different than "cure")
Faith	Trust
She or He	A human being of either gender
Home	Being with God, not in physical form
Energy	Life force, aliveness

Explanation of Concepts

The human personality contains many aspects, such as:

◊ Self concept

◊ Self-worth

◊ Relations with others

◊ Prosperity

◊ Career path

◊ Emotions

◊ Ability to speak out

◊ Truth or lying

◊ How we attempt to feel loved

◊ Ability to forgive

◊ Vindictiveness

◊ Ability to see how we're expressing who we are

◊ Sensitivity

◊ Need to control... and many more

These aspects are areas of ourselves that we may be refining. *"Refining"* means noticing aspects that need work, are missing, or are too dominant in our personalities. When we learn to reduce the intensity of our expression or avoidance of an aspect of ourselves, we are more in balance — we feel more in flow with life, less frantic. When we notice, understand and release an aspect that was not loving or helpful to us, one that was keeping us from feeling in balance, we have begun to heal that part of our personalities. Healing results in personal growth, refinement and development of our souls.

This is personal and soul growth. It is initiated by *"lessons,"* which are moment-by-moment events in our lives. Something happens and we react without realizing it. Events, conversations and emotions all come to show us which aspect of ourselves is out of balance. The lesson will come over and over until we notice where it is directing our attention. Noticing what's going on reveals new choices. They, in turn, create balance or further imbalance. We notice and learn from that, make new choices and begin to see more clearly the part in ourselves that we are refining. When we find an option that creates more balance, we can release the old way of thinking and reacting and embrace the reward of living a little differently. Here's an example. When I didn't know I was working on low self-worth and the ability to state my wants and needs, I attracted and accepted friendship from people who were completely absorbed in themselves. Not only would I not have offered a desire or opinion, they would not have asked for one. I was a silent audience for their "truths," willing to accept this appearance of friendship as the real thing. When I finally realized how lonely this setup made me feel, I began moving through my fear of being alone and ended all those relationships. I chose to be completely alone, rejecting new overtures of friendship out of mistrust of others and of my ability to pick caring friends. That was further imbalance. It revealed my need for refinement in being a good friend and team player. After many years, I decided to trust one woman and began slowly to express my needs in a relationship. This woman allowed me to experience balance in a relationship and confidence within myself. I have used this relationship as a foundation for further positive experiences with trust.

As I learned from my own life and watched the growth in my clients, the idea for this guidebook was born.

Why A Guidebook?

I enjoy jigsaw puzzles, partly because they are much like self-exploration. At first you're confronted with lots of little pieces that you'll have to put together to be able to make sense of the big picture. You begin with the tedious work of turning each piece over, color side up. At first it looks like chaos. Then you sort the straight-edged pieces and form the border, the safe container mentioned earlier. Once the puzzle is framed, you search out pieces that reveal the image that dominates the picture. It is like finding your central issue, and working on it first, usually because it's the most apparent or the most painful.

Some people stop exploring themselves at this early stage in the puzzle. Some stop a bit later, when the puzzle gets more challenging. But once you are committed, your heart urges you to persevere and you won't stop working at it until the whole picture emerges. You'll find smaller issues, smaller objects in the picture. You continue fitting pieces together until all that's left is blue sky or green grass. This part is really challenging! To fit pieces at this stage, you have to notice minute details. The work is slow, but you move forward as your eyes focus on the details you missed when you began the spiritual growth process. Your trained eye is more alert now. Pieces fall into place. The picture develops further. It becomes more meaningful. Frustrations of the past have less hold on you as you become eager to accomplish more. Your step-by-step successes on the path overcome the belief that "it can't be done."

Your choice to become fully conscious — as conscious as any person can become while still in human form — is the starting point for your puzzle. From there, listen to the urgings of your heart and educate your mind using the wisdom of the teachers you choose. Your life will change in subtle and intricate ways. You will change. This process is so subtle and organic that it will feel like it has always been a part of you.

Evolving Consciously

Becoming conscious doesn't mean you'll have dramatic psychic experiences, unless of course, they are part of your individual spiritual path. In fact, you may not have words to describe the changes happening within you, but the people who know you will tell you how different you seem. You may see their comments as mirrors reflecting your progress. However, keep in mind that when someone views you in a positive light, they can just as easily see you negatively. Neither reflection is the truth about you, it is only their view of who they see you to be. If you rely on outside opinions for validation, you will continue to draw lessons to you that slow your growth. What others say reveals who they are, even as they seek to define you. Your truth is inside you. As I'll discuss later, you learn your own truth by consciously noticing life, without judgment.

🕉 *Self-knowledge offers you a choice of behaviors that replace old automatic reactions.* Understanding and accepting an aspect of yourself is not the same as condoning or praising it. With compassionate self-knowledge, you are likely to see certain aspects of yourself for the first time. When you view a part of yourself clearly, without retreating in fear or disgust, its energy becomes available for transformation into a healthier, more productive state.

Paths Are Made by Walking offers no doctrine. Rather, I hope to offer you tools to set you free to find your own way, tools to consciously awaken and stay in tune with who and where you really are. I will to show you the goal — The way — and how your path forms in relation to it. What you do with the information is up to you.

Exercises

You alone must decide how much effort you are worth.

Throughout the book, you will find exercises to get you thinking and noticing. When you take the time to complete them, chapter by chapter, you will receive:

◊ Greater insight into your own process.

◊ Greater awareness of your old ways of thinking.

◊ A journal record of where you are today in the spiritual aspect of your personality. You can use this record to honor your progress each time you delve into fear, guilt or anger.

◊ Enhancement of your commitment to yourself and your spiritual growth.

The exercises are designed to enable you to explore what lies beneath your thoughts.

EXERCISE 1-1

A Blank Book

Find a blank book to use as a journal and companion to this guidebook. As you read, jot down concepts you agree with, disagree with, or don't understand. After reading this book the first time, look back through your journal and notice how you view the same concepts from this new perspective. With each additional reading, notice how you are developing a deeper understanding of the growth process. Since soul development is what living is all about, consider spiritual and personal growth to be the same thing.

Honor Your Individual Pace

Please work at your own pace, and in your own way, as you read this book. Use the exercises if you find them helpful. If you have been growing in self-awareness, perhaps you will allow the questions posed to deepen your search. You alone must decide how much effort you are worth. Remember, aspects of yourself, your unfinished business, your wounded places reveal themselves in layers. The process is a lot like cleaning out a wound as deeply as possible. If you don't clean it thoroughly, it will heal over, but remain damaged under the surface, causing long-term, low-grade pain. Similarly, life events have a way of calling your attention back to your emotional damage.

Being called back to similar painful situations, to recurring emotions, means you are strong enough to deal with the wound, not that you're doing something wrong. For example, when you find yourself once again feeling needy in a new relationship, your mind will tell you that you've worked on your neediness and that you "should be through it by now." But if you're feeling needy, you certainly aren't finished, filled or healed. In fact, the new relationship is exactly what caused you to re-enter that needy place to see what still calls out for healing. Just as you wouldn't tell a frightened child to go back to a dark room alone, don't tell yourself that your needs are inappropriate. When you notice that early injury, choose to offer instead your love and healing. When you have done "enough," the feeling of neediness will have transformed.

During the course of this book, I encourage you to notice and discard old ways of thinking and being that you haven't questioned before. The old ways are holding you back, slowing you down as though you were carrying a 100 pound sack of rocks on your journey through life. The sack gets caught on everything and puts a terrible strain on your back, but it's always been there, so you've never questioned its existence. Question it now. Discard it. Become lighter, freer, more flexible in your life.

A Few Words About Spiritual Growth...

The work you are doing as a spiritual being requires you to:

◊ Make a commitment to yourself

◊ Treat yourself with compassion

◊ Understand the spiritual growth process

◊ Be willing to love yourself

◊ Be patient

◊ Learn from your anger, judgments and resentments

◊ Understand and use the support offered by Divine guidance

I will discuss each of these in turn in this guidebook.

Spiritual growth is not about gaining occult powers or healing with crystals. If you're blessed with psychic abilities, like seeing auras or channeling spirits, I hope you use them with loving intention. But that's not the kind of spiritual growth I'm talking about here.

Spiritual growth is learning to expand beyond your old beliefs and rigid thinking, to grow larger and more open, to embrace the universe. It is an adventure, one filled with blisters, rock slides, clear mountain streams, the song of meadowlarks, rocks under your sleeping bag, and heavens filled with stars. All of these experiences, and more, are part of the journey. No single element defines the whole trip. If you are committed to the spiritual journey, it becomes an adventure filled with wonder and appreciation. Suffering is optional.

Chapter 1
Tools For Getting Started

- Your steps actually create the path. The path forms under your feet as you walk it.

- Self-knowledge offers you a choice of behaviors in place of old, automatic reactions.

- Being called back to similar painful situations, to recurring emotions, means you are strong enough to deal with the wound, NOT that you are doing something wrong.

2

Reincarnation

The path is long, long as life itself.

What Is Reincarnation?

Have you ever met someone with whom you felt an instant rapport, regardless of their age, gender or nationality? Have you ever fallen in love at first sight? Have you known a small child who couldn't get enough of trains, the Civil War, physical risks, certain animals or the like? Or have you known a child who was terrified, for no apparent reason, of bugs, or a certain color, of being alone, or of being in crowds? These strong likes and dislikes may well be unfinished business from past lives.

Reincarnation is the belief that the soul's identity remains constant as the body renews itself from lifetime to lifetime. It presents a way to understand the appearance of unfairness of life on earth. Believing that all souls are here to refine themselves and grow closer to God, and that all souls are at different stages in this growth and refinement process invites the acceptance that saint and sinner alike are doing exactly what they should be doing. (Much more on this concept later in this chapter.) All are equally beloved students learning at whichever level they are on.

Many cultures have accepted the concept of death and rebirth for millennia. They see life like a wheel — a circular path without end. And when people in these cultures die, the mourners' grief is eased by the knowledge that the wheel keeps turning, and that all souls will meet again and again.

Believing in reincarnation removes the sense of urgency from the spiritual refinement process. When we release ourselves from the drive to achieve spiritual perfection in a single lifetime, we free ourselves to find our own pace, without harsh self-judgment or fear of failure. We free ourselves to learn what our lives have to teach us.

Reincarnation as soul renewal is much like what happens with our bodies on the physical plane. Consider the rejuvenating properties of the human body. When we rub our arms, we flake away dead cells, but we don't become skinless. We naturally shed and replace cells continually throughout our lives. Our internal organs are constantly replacing themselves as well. In fact, in the course of a year, all the cells in our bodies will have died and completely recreated themselves. The actual cells are new, but only liver cells will replace dead liver cells, for example, so the organ's identity remains the same. Within a single lifetime, we are physically "reborn" again and again.

When we die, we shed the physical body itself, but the identity of the soul remains the same. Our souls retain the lessons we have learned — along with our emotional responses to those lessons — from every life we have lived. Much as a child matures on a physical level, so the soul matures on a spiritual level, from lifetime to lifetime, until it reaches oneness with God. That is the goal of the spiritual journey, our reason for being.

Until the 1960's, children generally were perceived of as "blank slates" that parents could write upon at will. Pregnant women exposed their fetuses to classical music, spoke to them in French and recited baseball statistics to them — all with the expectation that the child would retain this information and develop according to his parents' wishes. Reincarnation explains why, in spite of what a child's parent does, he will develop a personality all his own. The lessons he has invited and learned in all his previous lifetimes culminate in the personality he reveals in the present.

Parents who prenatally program their children haven't wasted their time in the big picture, however. There are lessons to be exchanged in all experiences. Perhaps the child is learning about being cared for or being awakened to a hidden talent. Perhaps through his rebellion to the programming, he is learning to speak up for his own desires and interests. There are so many potential benefits from a lesson that there is no point in judging it by its appearance.

Peace comes by flowing with your life experiences.

In truth, parents have committed long ago to the lessons they will teach — and the lessons they will learn — with their children, and their souls are aware of what those lessons are. Lessons are not about creating gifted musicians or linguists. They're about building character, inner strength, kindness, consideration and self-reliance.

It's impossible for the conscious mind to know whose soul is older, the parent's or the child's. Don't assume that a baby's soul is younger than yours. There is substantial wisdom in many, many young children. You can learn a great deal from them. Let go of appearances. Even the "willful" child could be showing you your need for patience or self-control. Certainly the "special needs" child offers opportunities to refine those aspects in yourself and then to teach them to the child.

Through conscious spiritual growth, we can shed old pain and regenerate ourselves mentally and emotionally. This spiritual growth process requires that we seek out and release whatever no longer serves the self. Once we have done that, the "old us" can die away, like old cells, and make room for new ways of being in the world. In this way, a new personality can take form without the physical body dying. We can evolve into better, more peaceful, loving people in this lifetime.

Consciously working on your personal growth accelerates the process of soul refinement. Lack of awareness of the spiritual journey is not negative, by the way. It's just an option — one that many people are experiencing. However, knowing that you have many lifetimes to become one with God can serve to remind you that you need not fear making mistakes on your spiritual path, that all choices are lessons for the soul, and that you can refine yourself at your own pace. This belief provides a framework for viewing events and relationships in your life. It answers the "why me, why now?" questions that can torment the mind for years. All this and more will be explored in this book.

Souls And the Creation of Lessons

Each soul is pure consciousness. Within the vehicle of a body, a soul experiences all human emotions, physical sensations, and of course, choices. Before a soul is born into a new body, it selects the lessons it wants to learn during that lifetime. The selections are based on what each soul knows it needs to refine or develop in itself.

For example, having been emotionally injured in one lifetime by an abusive or oppressive person, that soul would often select the same kind of relationships in the next incarnation. Why wouldn't the soul opt for loving companions in future lifetimes? The lessons brought by difficult teachers — the abusive, oppressive type — are created to teach how it feels to be on the receiving end of the misuse of power and how to stand up to it. Loving teachers don't bring those lessons and challenges. Take heart if your life seems difficult. You're busy learning a lot!

Can you imagine creating your own life lessons? Picture a place filled with souls working in small or large groups. In these meetings, individual souls are selecting lessons that they need to refine aspects of themselves. Before physical birth, in these groups, the choice of lessons is made and other souls agree to be part of that learning. Each soul, teacher and student, carries his or her own level of development. A soul may agree to teach you out of reciprocity (I owe you one for the help you gave me in the past), out of strength (I'll give you one because I've been through that learning and I know how to handle it) or even out of revenge (I'll keep you with me lifetime after lifetime until you atone for what you did to me in the past.)

How the lesson is brought reflects the development of the teacher. By learning and refining aspects of ourselves in this way, we elevate spiritually. It's like finishing the work in first grade and earning the right to enter second grade. The new level brings second grade lessons and many second graders—who are more mature than first graders. As you grow, you may notice that certain people are drifting out of your circle and that others are coming in. Or, your may be in "summer recess," where one group is leaving and you are feeling quite lonely. Trust that as soon as you've made room (by letting go of the old), the next level of teachers will begin to appear.

As souls, we do not have the power to decide exactly how the lessons will be taught. It's helpful to remember this. While a fellow traveler may agree to teach you, to play an important role in your life, how they do this is not predetermined. That is left to the teaching soul's free will. Imagine being pure spirit, not body, and having forgotten about how difficult life is within a body. Taking on many life lessons may seem appealing during "life review" with many loving, familiar souls surround you offering support. Yet each soul brings his or her unfinished business to the learning. Therefore, lessons may seem overwhelming when experienced in life. Since we don't remember our review time between incarnations once we reach physical form, we don't recall the contracts made or who is teacher and who is student. The teacher/student permutations are endless. Think about people close to you. You learn about yourself from the lessons they teach and about others by how they teach those lessons.

You might wonder whether someone treating you harshly is meant to teach you how to understand the misuse of power, or if your role is to act as a mirror for that person, reflecting for him the abusive aspect in himself that needs refining. Perhaps the relationship serves both purposes. Before taking in the intent of the lesson, the mind wants to know — to understand —

and it can latch on to this need for explanation for centuries. But holding on is not growth. Ultimately, the details don't matter. As you grow, you will accept and learn from what has happened to you and how you have reacted to it. Here's how to keep moving. ☺ *Note your reactions to events. Recognize which emotions you tend to dissolve into.* That approach sheds light on your wounded places. Healing them is spiritual growth.

If you let your logical mind lock you into the need for understanding rather than acceptance, you will create an endless series of questions, "Why me, why now, who's at fault, why here, why so severe, why all over again..." much like a 3-year-old child has a new question for every answer his parents devise. The 3-year-old stops asking not because he gets a satisfying answer, but because he gets bored with the game.

When you can, bypass your mind's ceaseless questioning and enter into your emotional response. Your ultimate job in spiritual refinement is to heal and move on. Understanding may appeal to the mind, but it is not necessary for healing. It is a trap that can keep you immobilized. It doesn't matter who said or did whatever. Look instead to your emotional response for guidance on what needs healing in you.

Karma

On a spiritual plane, the child's soul has come to learn. She brings into this lifetime a personality formed by unfinished business from past lives. The universal law of cause and effect (also called karma) dictates that eventually all within each self must be balanced. Karma means balance. If the child has not balanced an aspect of herself — such as her belief in poverty — in a past lifetime, she will have the opportunity to balance it in present and future lifetimes. Although she can't avoid any aspect of herself forever, there is little time restriction on working it through.

Naturally, the fewer aspects of her personality that she has learned about and refined through healing, the more difficult her path. Again, don't judge by appearances! An advanced soul may take on a very difficult lifetime for many reasons. Can you see how the mind can shut down forward movement until all this is understood? Yet so much on the spiritual plane is beyond human understanding and must be taken on faith.

Balancing aspects within the self means you complete both sides of a behavior so that you fully understand it and reap its rewards. Free will allows you to design the circumstances. Free will also allows the other to design his circumstances. For example, an unfaithful lover may not be betrayed himself in the same way or even in the same lifetime, but he will experience being betrayed at least once in his soul's development. Until this person's "betrayal" behavior is balanced, he will carry the unfinished lesson forward through as many lifetimes as necessary, repeating the roles of betrayer and victim. Depending on the methods his victims and betrayers choose to present the lesson, they also could throw themselves out of balance and require more lifetimes to refine their own reactions. Both teacher and student are responsible for their own actions and reactions. Even though lessons are offered in love, human reactions include guilt, fear and resentment, so lessons can leave us unbalanced. It is so complicated. Can you see why the need to understand just slows you down?

While you may be able to discover some information about past lives, the details aren't really important. They're only window dressing. Lessons, our emotional responses and our choices are what we are here to learn. Our emotional responses to how lessons are taught and our choices made in the heat of emotion are what we are here to heal. Life lessons exist to teach compassion. This is accomplished through the balance of experiencing both sides of behaviors.

Having been hurt yourself, you are less likely to hurt someone else, because you know how it feels. This is spiritual growth and the teaching of karma. The fellow souls who agree to teach the betrayer will probably include everyone he has ever betrayed. They may choose to join again in the role play in a new lifetime to present the lesson anew. On the soul level, the teaching is done with love — not human ego love of course, but each soul's love for the other, as children of God.

Reincarnation helps to put a painful childhood into compassionate perspective. Emotional, physical or sexual abuse damages a child's spirit, to be sure; on the physical plane, abused children are true victims. But on a spiritual plane, children are also souls who have invited certain lessons for this lifetime. When those lessons come early, and are taught harshly, children's emotions and spirits can be badly damaged. These children have more to overcome than those who were nurtured by gentle, openhearted parents, but if, as adults, they choose to work at healing their childhood wounds, they have much to gain spiritually. They could become very compassionate with other human beings because they know what it's like to suffer at the hand of another's cruelty. Or they may recognize the depth of strength and character they had to create for themselves in order to withstand the abuse, and draw on it to move ahead in their spiritual development. They may learn to speak up for their own needs because they've decided never again to take abuse from anyone. Souls grow through the difficult times.

All learning has value if the student has the eyes to see it.

Spirituality As A Lifelong Journey

Since being on a spiritual journey is your life, there is no point in setting deadlines. There is no end to spiritual development, just the journey. You don't need to worry about making mistakes on your path because each choice offers lessons. If you aren't satisfied with the outcome, you are free to learn from what happened and make another choice. You are also free to repeat your lesson the same way, over and over, hoping for something to change. Every choice is an option, each carrying no more weight than the other from a Divine perspective, but each carrying a different outcome.

Reincarnation presents a broad view which invites your mind to expand, to encompass more. A more open mind in turn reduces and eventually may eliminate fear from your life.

Fear takes up so much room in your mind.

Often there is so much fear that there is little room for much else and you feel frozen, with no options, no understanding. When fear dominates, you feel like a victim of life. In the framework of reincarnation, there are no victims, only lessons. Believing that we live again and again obliterates dead-end thinking (pun intended).

Know that you are ready for the learning you asked to experience in this lifetime. Lessons aren't learned in single events that, once experienced, will never recur. You are offered only what you are ready for—something your soul knows but your mind does not. Lessons can be so enormous and multifaceted that you may need to dedicate an entire incarnation to one way of being in order to learn.

For example, a woman learning to speak up for herself will create as many different relationships as she needs to help her explore victimization, develop her inner strength, and find her voice. She may experience an overbearing parent, a physically abusive husband, an angry child, know-it-all friends and rude salespeople all in one lifetime. Each teacher brings a version of the lesson in speaking up to abuse. Each interaction offers her a chance to feel the fear and make a choice—either stick with the old way of thinking and shut down, or start to uncover those inner resources and find her voice. She will begin to move forward once she recognizes her repetitive emotional response and her choices.

You have free will and can ignore the lesson a long time. You will take as long as you need to awaken. Teachers continue to bring the lesson until you no longer need it.

Because it can require several lifetimes to learn patience, honesty, gentleness or compassion, people's personalities develop differently. You literally see and hear life differently than the next person. You perceive and respond in a uniquely individual way. Your behavior is consistent with your perceptions until you decide to make changes in those perceptions. New perceptions pave the way for new behaviors. That is why, in the broadest sense, there are no victims, only students with free will who haven't understood the intent of a particular lesson yet.

Learning is impeded when you cling to the way in which a lesson is delivered. When you see yourself as a victim, when you hold resentments about the way a person acts toward you, or when you cannot forgive because you believe forgiving is condoning a behavior, you may be missing the intent of the lesson itself. Forgiveness releases you from the burden of hate and resentment. *(See Forgiveness, Chapter 12)* Your own soul, using the knowledge of what aspects of the self it needed to heal next, chose this lifetime's lessons. The circumstances of the teaching were designed by both you and the teachers of the lesson. ☙ *To stop feeling like a victim, learn to look for the lesson in each life event.* Understand the intent of the lesson; accept it, release it, forgive yourself and your teacher, and move on.

Spiritual Healing

This book will provide more detail about how to discover lessons and move forward. As an overview for now, the process of spiritual healing is represented in the following list.

1) Noticing that something or someone feels familiar.

2) Observing your emotional response to that person or situation.

3) Breathing into your feeling, enabling it to open and reveal itself to you.

4) Recognizing your emotional response earlier and earlier in interactions.

5) Beginning to see the pattern. Seeing which situations and with which kinds of people you feel this response.

6) Realizing what you know and what you have accomplished in your life. This helps you identify old ways of thinking that are no longer true or relevant.

7) Making a choice each time the old feeling reappears. The choice is between sticking with the old way of thinking or finding new options based on current strengths and knowledge.

8) Accepting that the person or situation comes to teach you about a part of yourself that needs to grow.

9) Using this awareness to accept the teacher's way of bringing the lesson. Forgiving the teacher through your understanding that on a soul level, the lesson is brought in love because you required the learning.

10) Releasing and letting go of emotional responses to the teacher, the lesson and how it was taught.

11) Making new choices by looking at situations and people differently.

12) Feeling gratitude for the teacher and for your awareness and growth.

The Power Of Gratitude

Gratitude completes the circle of healing. ✍ *After you have healed from a lesson, feeling grateful for it softens resentment and anger, speeding the process of releasing and opening to new lessons.* After all, wasn't it your own creative mind that drew to you all the characters and circumstances you needed in order to learn about and balance some aspect of yourself? Didn't these people, these fellow souls, agree to act out this event with you to help you do that?

And once you have achieved understanding and healing, aren't you qualified to assist other souls with the same lessons? Who is better qualified to teach about letting go and healing than someone who has just come through the experience? Since your soul's goal is to grow and refine itself, what could be better than helping another soul do the same? All souls are needed for the lessons they can teach. The more they learn about themselves, the better they are equipped to teach. So thank yourself, thank Divine Spirit, and ultimately you may be willing to thank even your harshest teachers.

Choosing To See Through The Eyes Of The Heart

This time around, become conscious of your choices. When you make a conscious choice, you can learn from it. Once you've completed a lesson, you don't need to repeat it. This means you understood it and healed from its impact. For example, when you are in the presence of a person you find unpleasant — like a rude grocery shopper who bumps you with her cart— you could try to uncover what you might be learning about that person and about yourself. Do you need to learn to see options? (One of which could be removing yourself from the situation.) If you automatically feel apologetic or defensive, do you need to learn to set boundaries with people who act aggressively (a misuse of power)? Or, if you automatically become enraged, are you being offered an opportunity to see the impact of your anger, to gain empathy with a shopper who bumped you while she was hurrying? Ask your heart to help you understand the lesson. Your mind will provide its own explanation, which will invariably be based on the need for control and looking good. You can see how limiting the mind's view is on the spiritual level. Your heart, in its quiet way, will reveal the purpose in this situation: why you, why now? Once you understand and heal your emotional response, this type of teacher will no longer come into your life.

> *When you look for understanding through the eyes of the heart, you can understand, accept, heal, forgive and move on.*

The process is so simple, but in the heat of daily living, it is easy to forget. The mind struggles and struggles with it. *Paths Are Made by Walking* will help you understand and practice this process in your life.

As you develop spiritually, you will find yourself growing less and less attached to day-to-day interpersonal issues. In the long-term, when viewed from a higher plane, daily crises are all so fleeting. Can you, for example, recall what upset you last year? Last month? How about yesterday's frustrations? From a spiritually developed viewpoint, there is no need to hold grudges, to remember insults and emotional wounding, or to hold others accountable for making you feel better. You can learn to bless all people, all situations, and move on.

Does this sound unwise, unlikely, or even impossible? For some, the task is beyond comprehension and for others, it is an intriguing possibility. Still others will nod knowingly. All these views are valid because all three represent the many individual learning levels. Let your response to these ideas — whether it is rejection, skepticism or acceptance — be a guidepost on your spiritual path. As you discover who you are as a spiritual being, you can see how far you have come. The closer you can keep your path aligned with The way, the easier it becomes.

Later in this book, you will learn more about how your spiritual growth helps others. For now, know that you are a soul who is here to teach other souls and to be taught by them. You have been here before, and so have they. You are not responsible for where others are in their learning processes. They are capable of learning only the lessons at their levels. You are not responsible for their poverty, their illness, or their aggressive natures. Each soul alone is responsible for his or her own path, a path chosen before birth, a path far beyond the mind's control. Allow others to witness what you are becoming: strong, courageous and personally responsible for all your choices.

You (like everyone around you) are on a spiritual path created by your own footsteps. No two paths are alike and all are equally valid. Remember that when you feel tempted to "correct" the footsteps another person is taking on his path. If it is your role to guide others in this lifetime, you will be taught how to do it without judging or correcting, rescuing or belittling. Your soul work must be done first. Be grateful for the opportunity to do it. Keep your own feet moving.

Chapter 2
Tools For Reincarnation

- Note your reactions to events. Notice which emotions you tend to dissolve into. That information sheds light on your wounded places. Healing them is your spiritual growth.

- To stop feeling like a victim, learn to recognize the lessons in life events. Learn to understand the intent of the lesson, accept it, release it, forgive yourself and your teachers, and move on.

- After you have healed from a lesson, feeling grateful for it softens resentment and anger, speeding the healing process.

3

Commitment

Until one is committed
there is hesitancy, the chance to draw back,
always ineffectiveness.

Concerning all acts of initiative (and creation)
there is one elementary truth,
the ignorance of which kills countless ideas
and splendid plans:

That the moment one definitely commits oneself,
then Providence moves too.
All sorts of things occur to help one
that would otherwise never have occurred.

A whole stream of events issues from the decision,
raising in one's favor all manner
of unforeseen incidents and meetings
and material assistance,
which no man could have dreamt
would have come his way.

I have learned a deep respect for one of Goethe's
couplets:

Whatever you can do,
or dream you can…. begin it.
Boldness has genius, power and magic in it.

W. H. Murray
The Scottish Himalayan Expedition, 1951

What Is Commitment...
And Why Is It So Hard To Make?

Being uncommitted to yourself is a lot like falling off a boat in the middle of a lake at night. Splashing wildly, choking on water, you struggle to stay afloat. In the same predicament, a person who is committed to life locates the light on shore and starts swimming. Commitment to yourself frees up your energy in much the same way. Rather than focusing on your fear of drowning, you focus on where you are going.

Making a commitment means that you will work toward growing and honoring yourself to the best of your ability no matter what. It's a promise to yourself that you absolutely intend to keep. It's a form of self-acceptance and self-love far deeper than fear.

Commitment is a concept foreign to many people. Americans in particular have learned to keep their options open; to discard the old and embrace the new. If you can't afford the latest trendy household gadget now, just wait six months and you're sure to find it at a garage sale. When I worked at a zoo years ago, I was shocked at how many overgrown Easter chicks and bunnies ended up as snake food because they became "too much trouble" for their owners. For many people, even marriage is a tentative commitment. Too many couples substitute "as long as we both shall love" for "as long as we both shall live" in their mental marriage vows.

Consider the commitments you've made in your life. How many of them have remained firm? Don't be surprised or discouraged if you haven't made any lasting commitments. Making a commitment to yourself may be the first truly steadfast commitment you will ever make, and certainly the most important.

Perhaps you were born into a family who emotionally or physically abandoned you. If so, you were taught that your thoughts and feelings were unimportant. When you felt pain, you were ignored, or perhaps you were punished more severely for complaining. In order to survive, you learned to ignore much of your own pain. You began to lose touch with yourself and your purpose. You learned to abandon yourself. Consider the failure rate in recovery programs. It is sizable not only because people don't commit to the recovery process, but because they don't know how to commit to themselves. You can't expect to be able to do something you were never taught! But you can learn!

I've noticed that many psychotherapy clients quit when the going gets tough. They have learned to avoid emotional pain. Their kind of commitment involves staying in the healing process as long as it's interesting and feels good. When they encounter emotional pain, they decide the treatment isn't working. They may blame their therapist, fellow group members, or their medication for the failure, but they quit therapy to stop the pain. This kind of contract is not commitment. A contract is an agreement to trade something of value only as long as both partners find it worthwhile.

Commitment encompasses many choices, but no escape clauses!

I don't mean you should stick with a therapist, group or medication when it feels to you like your pain is never-ending. The point is that once you are committed, you don't quit on yourself. The more you know yourself, the truer your assessment of what doesn't work for you.

In this kind of situation, when you're not committed to yourself, you might tell yourself that you're just so awful, just such a mess that no one could ever fix you. But once you've committed to loving yourself, to growing your soul, you'll take a more compassionate position. You'll be able to reassure yourself that even though the approach you tried doesn't work for you, you are going to find another way because you are worth the effort.

You'll know that *you* are still important and that as long as you need an outside source of support, as long as you need more tools to help you grow, you'll seek out the ones that are appropriate for you. Your commitment to yourself won't waver. You may look for a new therapist, or try different medications. You may join a church or start a women's support group. Perhaps you will start listening to audiotapes in your car, or go to a Zen center to learn to meditate. Only you know what truly suits you. If you're compassionate with yourself you'll discover what works for you through trial and error and through noticing your reactions.

When you're committed, you don't ever give up on yourself because your commitment is to you. Within your commitment to yourself, you will discover lots of choices, reactions, emotions, behaviors, standstills and indications of growth. If what you're doing for yourself isn't helping, it is not because you are so defective that nothing could work, but simply because that tool is not working for you.

How Is Making A Commitment Different From Setting A Goal?

Commitments and goals are entirely different. A goal is specific and time-directed. When you arrive there, it's over. Either you reach your goal or you fall short. Commitment is unending. You might establish goals within your commitment, however. For example, you might set a goal to spend six months or a year in psychotherapy learning about yourself. You might set a goal to go on three silent retreats a year, or to read a certain amount of spiritual literature, or to associate only with people who have kind natures. Those are goals. They are parts of the commitment, but the commitment itself is the umbrella over you, the unifying theme that makes sense of your life experiences.

Although commitment is not debatable or changeable, it's not rigid in an unhealthy sense because the commitment is simply to love yourself. I'm not advising you to love yourself in an egotistical, selfish, self-serving, hateful way. I'm talking about honoring yourself as an individual so that you can live your life in your own individual way.

Spiritual growth requires inner answers, unique to you. Have you ever noticed that when you go to someone else for emotional nurturing, you're always at least mildly disappointed? It doesn't seem to matter whether your confidante is spouse, parent, sibling or friend, because even though they give whatever they can, they give it in *their* way, and it doesn't quite fit. It isn't precisely what you need.

If it's not working, try something else.

The choices in life are like an all-you-can-eat buffet. When you look at the bounty that's on the planet, you see nearly unlimited choices. If you don't like one dish, just put it down and try something else. Don't ever accept anything that doesn't feel right for you. It doesn't matter why. You don't have to stop and analyze whether or not it's your neurosis making you run away. It doesn't matter because there are no mistakes. There are only lessons.

In spiritual growth, one size does not fit all. A central goal on your spiritual journey is discovering what fits for you. When you've committed to yourself, you'll begin to notice when something doesn't fit – some situation or some emotion — and you can begin attending to it sooner, dealing with it using your tools, coming to understand the lesson, healing the emotions involved, and moving on.

I encourage people who are consciously committed to their spiritual growth to explore a variety of tools and teachers. ☺ *Take what you like from each teacher you encounter.* But take *only* what is right for you. Get to know yourself well enough so that you're not swallowing someone else's under-standing whole. Knowing what you don't like, what doesn't fit you spiritu-ally, can be extremely valuable in guiding you toward what does work for you. It's your path; you have the right to choose where to set your feet.

If you start down a path that turns unpleasant for you and you don't like what you see, then you can start walking in a new direction. When you are committed to yourself, you make your path as you go along. Even if you don't know precisely where you are going, if you are committed, you can take a small step on your path and see if it feels right.. That's commitment. Suppose each step is a life lesson. If you take a step or two and you decide you're heading in the wrong direction because you don't like the conse-quences it brings, you've just learned something about yourself, because the path you cannot travel helps you recognize the one you can.

How Do You Know When The Time Is Right To Make A Commitment To Your Spiritual Development?

⊘ *The only way to love yourself is to be who you are, your authentic self.* You were drawn to this book for a reason. Either you are at a place where it's timely for you to begin the process in a new way, or you want an overview of what's possible. In a spiritual sense, you are exactly where you are supposed to be.

Just picking up this book is an indication of your readiness. The idea is to find out where you are. That's part of loving yourself. If you don't know where you are, you can't truly love yourself because you have only an imagined vision of who you must be. You're putting all your energy into being that image and projecting that image instead of being who you really are.

How Do You Make A Commitment To Yourself?

To make a formal commitment, simply say to yourself, "I'm willing to make a commitment to myself. I'm willing to be compassionate with myself. I'm willing to love myself. I'm willing to forgive myself." That's all you need to do to begin. It doesn't matter how old you are, how physically fit you are or how smart you are. It doesn't matter why you choose to make the commitment. There is no "too late."

⊘ *You may want to write "I hereby make a commitment to love myself" on a Post-it and stick it on a wall or mirror where you'll see it frequently.* Then when "life" happens to you, can remind yourself that you've made this commitment to look at things in a new way.

It's reassuring to know is that you cannot fail in your commitment to yourself. *You cannot fail.* Life lessons may seem difficult — and sometimes impossible — but there are no losers. There are no failures. God has infinite patience and an eternity to wait for us to learn our lessons. You may not be ready to give or receive unconditional love or total forgiveness. You may not be able to do that in this lifetime. That's fine. That's where you are. Grow from there. When spiritual teachers hold out only the ideal, you're left without the steps needed to get there. That's why a "how-to" guidebook can help you maintain your commitment.

When you center your commitment in yourself, you don't require yourself to live up to someone else's idea of spiritual development. When you commit to someone else's spiritual agenda, there's every chance that you'll fall short and feel like a failure. If that happens, there's a lesson to be learned. Rather than berating yourself for feeling less than perfect, you might try saying, "Boy, I learned a lot from that experience. First, I learned that I'm still looking outside myself for answers and approval. And, second, I learned that another person's path just doesn't work for me." You're not going to need to try out every guru or teacher before you understand that it doesn't work to buy someone else's spiritual agenda. I don't mean to say that you can't learn from heroes or gurus. Read and study anyone you want, but take only what you want. Don't swallow anyone's spiritual prescription whole. Remember, your commitment is to yourself.

You are learning to become you, not someone else.

Why Do You Need To Make This Kind Of Commitment? What Part Does It Play In Your Spiritual Development?

Once you make a commitment to yourself, you open yourself to the learning that is all around you. Your spiritual growth becomes your beacon. When you have that light to guide you, unnecessary distractions fall away. You begin looking at life as a series of lessons rather than feeling victimized by events. Commitment puts things in perspective. Commitment keeps you moving.

Once you make a commitment, your perceptions about life begin to shift. You see what's happening to you — a little at first, more so later on — as *helpful* events because they help move you forward, lighten up, grow strong. You let go of the belief that life is burdening you, or that you're being put upon in some way. You also begin to absorb the idea that a good and spiritual life isn't always happy and trouble-free. A spiritual life is whatever it is. (It's that simple.)

Commitment frees you to make new choices. You'll no longer feel bound to doing things in familiar ways just because that's the way you learned to do them. You'll begin to sort *yourself* out from all the extraneous training, education and attitudes that you may never have realized you had developed. It's as if you were removing layers of winter clothing and finding the "Spring being" inside of you.

Your mind is accustomed to running in certain pathways; ruts, if you will. Something happens and you respond in predictable way. ☙ *Open yourself to the concept that life is a series of lessons that are coming to you as gifts to help you grow your soul.* Then when life doesn't go your way and you catch your mind running through a familiar response, you'll switch it to a new response. "Oh, this is a lesson. I wonder what I need to know." Commitment serves as a tool to switch into new ways of perceiving the world. It's a gentle, loving way of perceiving the world and your life.

Once you make a commitment and you begin to perceive life as a series of lessons in spiritual development, the lessons are likely to come thick and fast. Making a commitment is a statement of willingness to learn. It's inviting the lessons. Here they come! Committing to learn, committing to spiritual growth, is likely to bring up the little demons that comprise unfinished business in your psyche. At the same time, when you hold life's lessons gently, examine them, learn them, and let them go, emotional pain becomes much less threatening. You start to clear out those stuck places one by one.

Using your new commitment to spiritual growth, you can begin to redefine pain as a tool rather than a weapon. Instead of running from pain, you can use pain as a road sign that guides you inward. I call it a healing crisis. Without the crisis to get your attention, you don't know that something needs healing. When you experience emotional or physical pain in the body, it's productive and loving to hold it gently and let it tell you what's wrong. If you had a young child who woke screaming from a nightmare, you would pick her up and soothe her. "What's wrong, what's wrong?" You wouldn't shut her away. You wouldn't say, "Your crying bothers me… I can't listen to it." You don't need to do that to yourself, either. You can ask yourself gently, "What's wrong, what's wrong?" and give yourself the attention you need to heal and grow.

When you recognize pain as a road sign that guides you inward, you'll be more apt to take a compassionate look at it. You can learn to grow beyond where you are by growing through the pain. Commitment insures that you won't as easily allow yourself to waste precious energy looking for ways to escape.

Healing is seeing with love what you once saw with fear.

One reward for learning a lesson is a new lesson. And since lessons are so often learned through pain, you are likely to resent them. It's human to feel resentment as a result of some of the process you'll go through on a spiritual path. You collected resentment during very difficult lessons. The key to moving forward is to discover the resentment and open to letting it go.

Resentment is normal. It's another one of those signals that you need to do a little housecleaning. If something happens and you find you're resenting it, not only do you have to resolve what happens, you also have to resolve the resentment, or it isn't finished. A large collection of resentments can lead to the tendency to slip into self-pity, "Look at all that's happened to me. I've tried so hard and I just can't get what I want." Self-pity traps energy that you could be using to move further down your path. The point is that you shouldn't be alarmed if you feel resentment. Resentment just indicates a need for more love. By loving yourself, you can see that when you are filled with resentment (and grudges), there is no room in you for something new. ☙ *Releasing resentments as they arise clears out room inside you for rewards from the Divine.* These rewards come in the form of new relationships, new opportunities, more awareness and understanding, and more inner peace. Be sure to collect your rewards!

If you can imagine yourself as a tapestry that is interwoven with the impact of your life experiences, then picture yourself gently pulling out old, defective threads and re-weaving new stronger threads. Tapestries are intricate patterns with many warps and wefts. When you change single threads, you alter the whole design, even though it may be invisible at first to the outer eye. As you carefully and lovingly repair your tapestry, you are creating a personalized, unique and beautiful pattern. This gentle technique feels safe and subtle. Growth and changes experienced this way feel natural rather than jarring.

Chapter 3
Tools For Commitment

❧   If it's not working, try something else.

❧   Take what you like from each teacher you encounter.
But take only what is right for you.

❧   You may want to write, "I hereby make a commitment
to love myself" on a Post-it. Put it up where you'll see it
frequently.
Then, when life doesn't go your way, you can remind
yourself that you've made a commitment to look at
things in a new way.

❧   Life is a series of lessons that are sent to help you
grow.

❧   Releasing resentments clears out room inside you for
rewards from the Divine.

The Process
Of
Spiritual Growth

The universe is following your instructions.

What is the process of spiritual growth? It's like the stages of physical maturation in which a baby first crawls, then stands, walks, and finally runs. The baby's body instinctively knows what the next step is and begins reaching for it long before he has the capability to achieve it. And your soul is undergoing a similar kind of evolution. No matter what you do or think consciously, your soul is experiencing growth and development. When you bring the process to your conscious awareness, you begin to accept the events in your life as "lessons" designed to promote soul growth. In this way, you can see them as gifts rather than punishments.

The process, then, becomes one of noticing a certain lesson, learning from it, letting go of your emotional resistance and your reaction to it and opening to the next lesson. It may require an entire lifetime to learn a lesson that is particularly difficult for you. The same situation keeps coming up, again and again, often in more subtle forms. It can be brought by any person and usually by many people. Each one acts as a teacher and brings his or her version of the lesson.

All of this noticing, by the way, is usually done by looking backward. Until you get into the habit of finding lessons, you'll see them only as patterns, in retrospect. For example, if your friends use you the same way, that's a pattern. What are they each teaching? Your lessons could be:

◊ That it hurts to be used (so you won't use others).

◊ That you need to love yourself enough to find new friends.

Once you know the lesson, you'll spot it more easily whenever a teacher brings it. As you clear out current lesson-bringers, you make room for new teachers. You will be given many opportunities to practice your new skills of perceiving one-sided friendships and wanting more for yourself.

Most people get stuck here. They focus on appearances rather than lessons within an overall process. ☻ *But if you're aware that there is a process at work moving you along the spiritual path, you begin to look at events as things that have been brought to trigger any unfinished business in you.*

How Does It Work?

Much as time lapse photography has shown us flowers coming into full bloom in a matter of seconds, our society has encouraged us to believe that we can have whatever we want almost instantly. We have instant-on TV, instant mashed potatoes, and Velcro closures on shoes. Spiritual growth is not like that. It happens at a pace unique to each person. As Mohandas Ghandi said, "There is more to life than increasing its speed." The moreness comes in slowing it down so that you can be truly present in life... so that you can eat a plate of food and actually see the colors, smell the aromas and taste the textures rather than wolfing it down in front of the TV, then prowling for ice cream because you don't feel satisfied.

It's helpful to know that the Divine Spirit is infinitely patient. There is no deadline for achieving spiritual refinement. You have lifetimes to learn. But you can *choose* to become conscious of your lessons — to recognize them, learn from them, let go of their emotional charge and move on to the next level of spiritual development. This choice moves the process along more easily.

The process of spiritual development is like the earth's movement around the sun. You don't see the movement or think about it, and you don't consciously cause the sun to rise every morning and set every night. When you do notice it, you may be awed, but you don't worry about it. You don't wonder what it's doing over Argentina right this minute, or think about when its rays touch China. You don't assume that on a cloudy day, the sun is gone and is never coming back. The process is always there. You can't control it so you've learned to *trust* it.

Moreover, if you believe that you should be able to finish your spiritual growth quickly and get on with the rest of your life, here's the bad news:

The elevator to spiritual refinement is broken. Please use the steps!

Spiritual development requires commitment and work. The only way to insure real change is to accept your individual spiritual process as your life's work. I don't mean to say that everyone should become a holy person. Some people will live on communes, others will work in shops, offices or factories. Some will be mothers or school teachers. Others will be skin divers, while still others will be tarot card readers. There are all kinds of ways of doing it, all kinds of paths. There's no right way and no wrong way. Everyone on a spiritual path can live in the world by incorporating spirituality into every aspect of daily living. Whether you're a banker, a baker or a hula hoop maker, your purpose on earth is to learn the lessons that refine various aspects of your soul.

Starting On A Spiritual path

So how do you know where you are spiritually? Look for clues in how you relate to yourself and the people around you. Let's say you're with someone on a regular basis, in either a personal or business relationship. That person always startles or disappoints you with his behavior, yet his behavior is always the same. When you recognize the repetition in that situation, you know you're not yet living in a conscious way. That person isn't changing, so why are you startled or disappointed when he does the same things he's always done? Expecting people to be different than they are is a good place to notice your need to become conscious; the only person you can change is yourself.

An early step in spiritual development is defining what you want for yourself. No one outside yourself can really know what you want. You may want a Mercedes, or a job in a Fortune 500 company, but those aren't the kinds of desires I'm talking about here. I'm talking about intangible desires. I remember years when all I wanted was to survive – just to get through the day. And that's exactly what I got. Nothing more. When I finally realized that what I wanted most was inner peace, I began opening up spiritually. For more than ten years, that desire has carried me through much personal pain and brought me closer to making inner peace my daily reality.

EXERCISE 4-1

What I Know Already

If knowing or expressing your inner desires is difficult for you, consider what you give others. People often give others what they desire for themselves. Do you want love, consideration, respect? List your inner desires in your journal. Do this by completing the sentence "I want..." as many times as you can.

If you are adept at stating your desires, try the next step, which educates you about your readiness to accept what is happening in your life. Think about problems in your life right now. Your issues with matters like relationships, work, addictions and fears are the subject matter of your individual process. Begin these sentences with "My issues are..."

Changes in the way you feel about your issues are evidence of your progress. Can you say that you accept what life brings you because you trust that it comes for your highest good? First, you need to learn to want. As you start to fill up, the wants will soften to preferences. Ultimately, when you are consciously moving along your path in trust, you will begin to accept what life brings. I want, I prefer, I accept. But please be completely honest with yourself about where you are. Don't fake it or force it. Allow yourself to be where you are.

Ask...

Perhaps the simplest way to begin awakening to your spiritual process is to ask Divine Spirit for the awakening to begin. When you ask, you set the process in motion. You can't dictate what's going to happen first, but once you set things in motion, stopping the process may feel worse than continuing. This is because you will be more aware of how you've been limiting yourself. As your soul awakens, longing for growth increases. You become aware that you want something more from life, that your life has more meaning than you've been allowing yourself to see. So you ask God to put your feet on a spiritual path in a conscious way. Once you ask and commit to keep growing, you'll expand and open to a much larger universe than you ever dreamed possible. You'll move one step at a time.

It can be uncomfortable to ask because it's very likely that you've been taught not to ask for what you want. Many of us have been taught not to be a bother. Try looking at asking in a new way. Asking is reaching out and opening yourself to receive. Asking is not about demanding or holding on. It is about staying open while bits and pieces of information come together. It is about accepting what appears and trusting that in time you will understand and make the connections for the highest good of all involved. Spiritual asking doesn't emanate from fear or aggression. It comes from a deep willingness to know, to listen and to receive.

You may be one of many people who believe their prayers are never answered. Perhaps you were taught to create affirmations and to ask God for exactly what you want. "Oh Lord, won't you buy me a Mercedes Benz?" You asked God for what you wanted, but He didn't deliver immediately. A universal law in spiritual development is holds that when you ask for what you want, the wheels are set in motion to deliver it, but only when you become ready to receive. You may well have asked for something that you won't be ready to receive for a long, long time — not until you've refined your soul in preparation for what you desire. This pertains to both tangible and intangible desires. Beyond that, you may find that your desires change as you move through your life lessons and into more advanced levels of spiritual development. Stay in touch with who you are and what you want because Spirit lovingly clears out the blocks to make you ready to receive what you have asked for.

When you ask for something, it's not like I Dream of Jeannie crossing her arms, bobbing her head and making it happen. You invite in lessons and the lessons come. You're challenged with everything you've been afraid of about those situations, about those kinds of people. You're given unlimited opportunities to look at all the wounded places you have inside, to heal them, and to move on. Asking uncovers what's in the way of your receiving. First things first!

Ultimately you will attain your goal.

Be Still And Listen, Respect And Heal Yourself

"I am a human being, not a human doing"

It can feel really hard to do nothing, to wait in silence, listening for that "still, small voice within." How you learn to wait is part of your response. Imagine throwing a handful of pebbles into a swimming pool. When you race to gather them, the turbulence you create prevents you from finding them. Once you stop trying so hard, the water becomes calm and you can find the pebbles easily. You learn your own flow, what works and what keeps you from your desires.

Culture teaches us that keeping busy, being productive and being in a relationship are our primary value to society. Spiritual development flows from allowing your perception of life to slow down dramatically so that you can be more aware of your own flow. So that when you have a feeling, when you have a physical sensation, you can deal with it by staying open and aware.

If you leave a troubling encounter with another person and just go away and get terribly busy, you won't learn anything new. But if you're committed to being on a spiritual path, then as soon as you are alone, you can go inside and deal with it. You can honor your feeling, open it up, explore it. How is the feeling explored? ☺ *The simplest way is to breathe into the feeling.* Let's say I'm talking with someone and I notice that I have my arms crossed over my solar plexus and my stomach is twisting into knots. If I breathe into that area, the feeling will open. It will reveal itself to me. Fear will warn, "Don't touch that subject! It's dangerous. There's something wrong here." When you go inside, you learn whether the fear message is true right now or if it's old, unfinished business. Most often you'll discover a release of energy that comes in the form of tears or a deep sigh. It's something you might want to do alone, with a friend or a counselor.

Say you're talking to someone, and you breathe into your feeling, and you realize you're feeling attacked by this person. Now that you're aware of it, you have choices.

Awareness replaces powerlessness with choices.

In this moment, you may ask yourself, "Do I want to stand here and continue experiencing this? Do I want to speak up to the person and tell him not to talk to me like that? Do I want to say, "I need to go now, I'll talk to you later," turn, and leave, all without getting into an argument, or explaining, or making up excuses, but just allow myself to leave?" Once in your office or in your car, allow yourself to get back into your feeling and explore it privately. Or wait for your counseling appointment. Or call a caring friend and talk it out with her.

You don't have to do the healing right in the moment. Later, when you talk about something that was an emotional trigger for you, you will feel it again. Our tendency is to ignore the feeling, to numb out and try not to feel it. But when you're ready to breathe into that feeling, it will reappear and you'll feel like the danger is right in front of you. It can feel as potent as the original trigger. So wait for a safe time and place.

You also need to realize that you have lifetimes of these repressed moments of awareness hidden in your body. Whoever angers you today may be triggering something that's been hidden in you for decades. Therefore, your emotional response may be bigger than the current situation warrants.

Notice and honor your emotions when they appear, then go inside and discover what generates them. When you respond to a situation with charged emotions, recognize it as unfinished business. When you look at the unfinished business with compassion, you have an opportunity to heal it, understand your emotional reaction, your process, and then move beyond it. When the situation comes along again, you may find your response lessening each time. This is a helpful way to assess your progress.

Feelings are very important. Over time, you'll be growing toward a place where you'll react less emotionally, but until then, strong emotions help you uncover the work you need to do. ☺ *The emotion is the signpost pointing inward. It tells you that something wants your attention, something is unfinished.* If you can go inside with compassion and without judgment, and look at it, you can understand it and begin to heal that aspect of yourself. As you grow, you'll find yourself less and less charged about the issue, less emotionally hooked by it.

You'll know that you're growing spiritually when your perceptions about your emotions begin to shift. The first shift happens when you have an emotional response to an event and you think, "Oh, there's an emotion, I'm sad, I'm angry, I'm feeling attacked. What's my going on? What am I learning? What needs my attention?" For example, take someone who is in a relationship where her stomach hurts all the time. That's definitely an issue she could look at, but she ignores it. The pain gets worse as her body strains to tell her that she is in an unhealthy situation. When she recognizes the pain in her stomach as a message to be heeded, she has made the first shift. When she connects the relationship with the pain, she's made another. When she is able to honor her pain and leave the relationship or speak up about it, she's made still another shift. Perhaps months or years later, she comes into contact with a person who is much like the person in that original relationship. If she recognizes that this is a similar kind of person, and that this time she didn't respond emotionally – instead she went away feeling good and competent and didn't lose any self-esteem in the process – she realizes that she has completed that particular lesson. Her stomachache was the guide.

I don't mean to oversimplify the process. Nothing is ever resolved in one go-round. You'll go through it again and again and again, like a spiral moving through layers. Events creating emotional responses have happened more than once. The first time, you're cleaning out boulders, then rocks, stones, pebbles, and ultimately you're cleaning out sand. It's really hard to pick up sand because it's so fine, but a single grain is as irritating in your eye as a boulder is on your foot. As you become more spiritually refined, you will be more sensitive to whatever remains unfinished in you. And this will move your process along, inviting more experiences of the lesson.

You can see why commitment is so important. Commitment involves taking the time to notice and honor where you are and what you're experiencing, and then with compassion, support your response so you can open it up and take a look at it. Most of us would rather take that antacid or get real busy and not notice the stomachache.

Start small, stay present in your own life and listen for your inner wisdom. When you come to see a fact as it is and don't let your fear distract from it, you will no longer meet disappointments, only events. This is a peaceful place to be in your spiritual growth. This is where your process can take you.

Release The Negative

Once you begin to hear how many negative comments you make to yourself as you walk through your day, you will be amazed that you could live with that much abuse going on in your head. Anything negative that anyone said to you while you were a child, or that you think now, judges your adult self – you're clumsy, too sensitive, stupid, in the way, not good enough. It is all stored in your head and energetically in your body. When you begin to hear those messages, you have choices. You can begin to throw them out, one thought at a time. Imagine putting those negative thoughts in helium balloons and sending them upward, flick your fingers away from your body and send negativity into the center of the earth, send negative voices to their room, or put them in an imaginary locked box. Let God dissolve them for you.

Be aware that every time you think one of those negative thoughts, it's an affirmation that you're putting out in the world. Thoughts are things. The universe responds by saying, "If that's what you want, that's what you shall have." So when you say, "Why does my life never change?" or "Why do I always have trouble?", listen to what you're saying. Why say "trouble always finds me," or "I'm getting sick."? Start releasing the ownership of all that negative stuff. Allow the possibility of some positive flow.

The following activity will help you gauge how negative your thinking is.

EXERCISE 4-2

Checking Into Your Negativity

Imagine that you start each day with $100 worth of energy. Each time you have a negative thought, write it down and deduct $10. At the end of the day, see how much money you have left. Did you bankrupt yourself with negativity before you got out of bed? Try this exercise every day for a week.

It will show you how negative thoughts and emotions can rob your life of pleasure, joy and energy. Don't let your fear mind beat you up for having negative thoughts! Your job is to notice what's there and to begin to release a decades-old habit. It will take awhile. So, release those judgments, one thought at a time.

Just like a computer that has been programmed a certain way, the mind does not distinguish between whether what we're telling it is the truth or a lie. It accepts all of our negative input as valid data, which is stored and fed back to us every time we press the key that says we want the data released. When we begin to put in positive data about ourselves, things like "I am lovable and capable, I am a beloved child of God, I have value and worth," the fear we hold in our minds will say, "That's not true! The other stuff is true. I've been programmed with this other stuff for decades. Don't tell me this new stuff because I won't accept it!" Think of releasing the negative first as clearing your memory banks. We have to make room for the new data.

Our behavior is based on how we think. We run our lives on either the positive or the negative assumptions of the truth about ourselves. Once we have a theory, our minds will do everything in their power to prove that theory. If we think someone is unfaithful, we will find theater tickets and strands of hair and all kinds of clues to prove that theory. The person we suspect may in fact be completely innocent. We'll do the same thing with ourselves. We say, "Just my luck. I never win." We turn our beliefs into realities without even seeing the process. If we think we're less than intelligent, we'll pick easier courses, study less and not excel. If we think we're unlovable, we'll support that by acting in unlovable ways so we won't welcome any friendship. It's not a conscious act. It's something we do before we "wake up" and know that we have choices.

Your commitment to spiritual growth becomes essential when you begin to realize that you have so much work to do. It can be quite a blow to realize that you've allowed this pain to go on for so many years and been this abusive to yourself. It can feel overwhelming to suddenly realize that there's so much unfinished business and so much negativity when you thought you were pretty much "finished." Please realize that we don't get finished. That's the process. It's ongoing. And it doesn't all happen in one lifetime. The whole purpose of each lifetime is to learn and grow and develop as much as we choose. Then we come back again and do some more. If you are not comfortable with the concept of reincarnation, commit to doing all that you can in one lifetime. Commit to finding your joy.

Transformation involves dismantling of the old ways as well as creation of the new. ☯ *You must be willing to let go of the old ways of being and thinking in order to make room for new ways.* Think of yourself as a bowl full of muddy water. As you begin to awaken spiritually—through activities like studying, practicing, listening to teachers – you pour spoonfuls of clean water into the dirty water. Each spoonful makes little impact on its own. That's why self-transformation can take lifetimes. However, when you are open to releasing and letting go of everything that isn't loving and productive in your life, you empty the bowl first. When you do that, the bowl is ready to be filled with clean water. Don't expect this emptying and refilling process to be easy—fear will fight against letting go as fiercely as a junkyard dog. Spiritual growth is simple, but it's not easy.

Let's Replace Negative With Positive

Using Affirmations

If you use affirmations, be sure to use them consciously. Use present tense and use the affirmation positively. Avoid the use of "I hope" or "I will." For example, you might affirm, "I am a relaxed person." There is no value in using negative affirmations like, "I don't overeat." Make affirmations about your inner state, not about external situations like jobs or relationships. You cannot control anyone or anything other than yourself, your observations and perceptions. We are not here to change others. We serve as our brother's teacher not his keeper.

Try using your affirmations for two to three weeks before committing to them formally. How realistic are they in your life? If you're affirming an hour of meditation time each day and you have young children, is it possible to set aside that much time? If you affirm that your heart loves everyone, is that realistic in your situation? Instead, you might try, "I'm learning to love."

Trust Yourself

Learn to know yourself through your body. Sleep when you're tired. Naps are great; use them when you need them. Eat when you're hungry. Use the toilet when you need to. Awaken your senses and experience your life through them. Smell your food. Feel the fabrics you wear. Let music vibrate inside you. Listen to your heartbeat. Trust your body.

Begin To Sort Your Experiences In A New Way

As you become more aware of your own process and begin to become more compassionate with yourself, you will see how different experiences and people effect you. If an experience contributes to your well-being, it's probably right for you. If it hinders self-development, it's not loving and helpful. Begin to choose in favor of yourself rather than letting other people and situations direct you. Remember the last time you said yes when you felt like saying no — you stayed late to finish a project, or baked cookies or sat up reading a book recommended by a person you didn't admire.

Fear drives us to put ourselves last or one-down. We fear how others will perceive us, or that we are the only ones who can do what's been asked of us, or that someone will be angry with us. The fear of *potential* misfortune drains our energy and saps our spirits. This is not compassion.

Instead of depending on others for guidance, tune in to your own reaction to what's happening. Know your bottom line in advance and hold to it as firmly as you can. Everything can bring learning if you look at it with learning in mind. From this vantage point, lessons become events to refine your unfinished business. They stop being do-or-die situations. When you see life as a stream of events flowing inward, bringing many opportunities to learn about your old ways of thinking, a missed opportunity to maintain a boundary, to say no, or to speak up becomes only that — a missed opportunity. There will be more — as many as you require.

How You Do It Is How You Do It

The more you participate in your life, the more you get out of it. The same principle applies to spiritual growth. In your search for intellectual understanding of spiritual matters, do you seek a guru to prescribe the "appropriate" spiritual path for you to follow? Many people do make that choice, but signing up for someone else's path is like getting on a railroad spur rather than staying on the main line. You can do it if you want to or need to. It can slow you down, but there's no ultimate damage done because there are lessons to be learned there, too. If you need to give over your power and conscious awareness to another human being and let them be in charge of you for awhile, there's a lot to be learned from that for both of you. I doubt that many of us can succeed in our growth without teachers, but be aware that one person does not have all the answers for you. He may have answers for himself, but not all the answers. Anybody who has achieved perfection is no longer on the planet!

When you begin to become conscious and slow your thoughts down enough, you become more aware of the details of what's going on, and you'll discover a tendency to respond, or to do things in a specific way. That's your way. Honor that. Do only what you can do in the present moment. Let each step you take teach you what step to take next.

Ask Divine Spirit to show you which practices will enhance your growth. You will be drawn to what works for you. Schedule time for your spiritual practice each day. If you don't make room for yourself in your schedule, fear will keep you busy, putting everything else you have to do ahead of spiritual practice. The amount of time you practice is as individual as you are, so flow with what feels right for you and expect the time period to adjust as you grow. Practice is essential to staying on track. And although spiritual practice doesn't make "perfect," it does make progress. When you follow your spiritual practices, stay awake and aware. Rote chanting and mindless rituals don't enlighten. Look for spiritual practices that you like to do for their own sake, not to achieve specific outcomes. The great athletes are the ones who love to practice. As golf pro Ben Hogan once said, " The more I practice, the luckier I get!"

Keep it simple. Slogans and clichés can have real meaning. If the practice you design for yourself is too long or difficult, or doesn't fit who you really are, you're unlikely to keep at it. Don't be concerned when your practice changes. It will change as you evolve. That's in the process. If something falls away, just know that something new is coming. You'll learn many lessons in flexibility, as well as in patience, courage and love. If something doesn't work, try another way. Ask your inner guidance and something will show up. Be alert for all the little miracles that appear once you set your intention to grow spiritually. Don't expect fireworks, just tiny reminders that Divine Spirit is with you.

Remember, this is your spiritual journey. You will begin to gather bits of information from many sources. Ultimately, the spiritual fabric you weave will be uniquely yours.

Let Go Of Fear

When you focus on growth, you begin discovering your real self by peeling off the false identities that have kept it hidden. You move forward by letting go, but as you strip away your various facades, fear leaps forward to protect them. Remind yourself that you're letting go of what's false to make room for what's true. ☺ *True freedom comes from letting go.* When you try to let go, you may be surprised at how firmly you cling to the old ways of being and believing. All the old control issues, all the doubts well up inside. You may find many reasons to stay the same. Fear is a powerful inhibitor. If it scares you enough and convinces you that it can keep you safe, you're stuck. Fear confuses. It blinds you to what is truly possible. If you don't immediately see a way out, it doesn't mean a way out doesn't exist.

When you begin to hear your own thoughts and become aware of your behavior in the process of daily living, notice how much fear is present. The thinking mind, which I call the fear mind, seeks information about everything. It is driven exclusively by fear. It will never have enough information to be satisfied. You can never fill it with enough information to quiet it. Let me describe how that can slow you down and confuse you. You go inside and find a feeling, such as fatigue. You say, "What's going on here?" Fear mind would say, "Why do I feel this way? I don't know. Well, then, I can't do anything about it. I can't move until I know why. I have to know why." That's the fear mind keeping you stuck, because you may never know why. If you answer fear mind logically, "I feel this way because I feel threatened in the presence of this person," the response flies back, "Why do I feel threatened?" It becomes a whirlpool sucking you down into "that's not good enough, there is never enough information, I will not let you move forward until there is more information. Find out more about... How many people have studied in this way? How many people have journaled? How many men and how many women? How did they get there?" This is fear mind telling you not to trust what you're drawn to, what you know to be true.

If you're drawn to journaling, your heart wants you to journal. If you're drawn to meditating, your heart wants you to meditate. Fear says, "Wait a minute." Fear's goal is to stay in charge. And it does that by hinting or screaming at you, "There's danger here! You know people have gone crazy while meditating? You know people have left their bodies and never been able to get back in again? Do you realize how dangerous this is? And time... do you realize how much time this self-indulgence will take?"

The heart says, "You need some peace and quiet
so that you can hear my small, still voice.
You need some silence."

Society (and fear mind) says, "You're a worthless wreck! You're sitting around the house doing nothing when you should be going to church or reading the Bible every day, or chanting religiously." The heart says, "Do it the way that feels right. Do it the way that enhances your inner peace, not the way that keeps you stirred up all the time." Fear is quite a roadblock and you may not yet realize how much it is present in your every action.

When you ask endless questions, you may feel like you're setting up a safe approach for a new spiritual practice, but really it's the fear mind keeping you stalled. Your heart will never lead you wrong. I don't mean your romantic heart, but your heart that is the voice of God within you. It will never lead you wrong. There is no danger. Keep checking in with that inner wisdom. Let's not tiptoe cautiously through life only to arrive safely at death.

Fear mind is a barrier to the heart. And it has a much louder voice, so it's heard much more frequently. The fear mind originally had a protective function, but it ends up controlling you. Once you listen to your heart, to the still small voice within, it will let you know when to stay in a situation and when to leave. You really don't need the fear mind for anything anymore. It once taught you to look both ways before crossing. But if you could in fact be totally attuned to your heart, you wouldn't let yourself be hit by cars; you would act from self-love rather than fear and avoidance.

Here's an example. When I get on a highway, I often affirm, "God goes before and makes smooth my way." When I say this out of trust and let it go, traffic flows and the trip is easy. When I see brake lights and say this affirmation out of panic or an effort to control, I find myself stuck behind all the big trucks and slowpokes. When I go in faith, the rewards are frequent. When I squeeze my spirit, trying to make life conform to my wishes, all I get is headaches!

Fear mind is the ego. The ego wants job security. The ego says, "Don't listen to God, listen to me. I will never lead you wrong. I live here on the planet. He doesn't. He's up there in heaven. He's got too many people to worry about. He's not looking at you. He's not helping you. Look how He lets people be hurt in wars and starve to death. He doesn't really care. Listen to me. I know what's best for you." And our culture supports that belief by urging you to gain control of your world through planning, barred windows, and zillions of choices that allow you to keep everything the same so that it doesn't upset your view of life.

The stated goal of the spiritual path is to get beyond the ego. The thought of an ego-less mind scares some people, but it really just means that your will for yourself and God's will for you are the same. Listen and learn to differentiate between the times when God is talking and when your ego is controlling. Get in touch with a feeling in the moment. Allow its energy into your overall flow. You will find yourself feeling stronger and more creative. You will get bigger, not smaller, because you will have access to more of yourself. It's not about win/lose. It's about win/win.

Divine justice is so much broader and deeper than the human mind, which sees only the surface, can understand. You say, "it's unfair, it's wrong," without knowing what's going on beneath the surface, what God has to offer. You can't look at another human being and know what his lessons are or her path is. The more you can let go of needing everyone to do life a certain way, the freer you become to live your own life.

People go through life's journey with a lot of baggage. It is helpful to see what you've been holding onto because to move forward, you must discard something. Look at how you have been judging yourself. There is a difference between what your heart knows is true and what fear mind tells you. Release the "not-true." When you do this, you elevate your energy to a higher plane and open yourself to receiving new information and new ways of being.

Author Anais Nin wrote of a time when she realized that the risk of remaining tight in a bud was more painful than the risk it took to blossom. Your commitment and intention will bring you to that time. Compassion for yourself will speed the process.

EXERCISE 4-3

Lightening Your Fear Load

Circle one or more of the fear traits listed in this exercise. You'll be drawn to the ones that best describe where you have work to do. Refining these traits is what your lessons are all about. Suspend judgment. Ignore the uncircled items for now. Work only with what you are ready to release right now. You'll be ready to release other characteristics and behaviors when the time is right for you. This process is ongoing so it takes as long as it takes. It will probably take your lifetime.

If you feel stuck anyplace along the way, tune in to any judgments you're making. Release judgment of yourself first. Judging the self leads to judgment of others, of ideas, of institutions, etc. Release judgment every time you encounter it. Don't judge yourself for judging! Just notice it, release it and move on. This is the process of healing and growing spiritually.

Remember, the traits you circle show you where your work lies. Notice and release one trait at a time until you feel freer.

Fear Traits

judgment	boredom	doubt	apathy
lack of focus	perfectionism	pride	procrastination
fatigue	inadequacy	greed	depression
anger	self-loathing	grief	hatred
abandonment	rejection	envy	resentment
jealousy	guilt	shame	victimization
blame	dishonesty	denial	need to control
ambivalence	indecision	fear of intimacy	alienation
fear of disappointment	self-criticism	criticism of others	unworthiness

Chapter 4
Tools For The Process Of Spiritual Growth

❧   Look at events as things being brought to trigger any unfinished business in you.

❧   Explore your feeling by breathing into it.

❧   An emotion is a signpost pointing inward. It says something wants your attention, something is unfinished.

❧   Let go of the old ways of being in order to make room for new ways of being.

❧   Freedom comes from letting go.

❧   Release judgment every time you encounter it

Compassion: Be Gentle With Yourself

Trusting self, foibles and all, with love, is essential, because love is not just for others.

Much as the Earth's pressure compresses coal into diamonds, your life lessons forge precious strengths within your personality. And like mining for diamonds, you have to dig deep to discover these rewards for your hard work. If your thinking is rigid and you remain loyal to your old beliefs, you'll never find the diamonds deep within yourself. Mining these gems calls for new ways of thinking and being. ✤ *If you choose to open your mind and look at your injured places with compassion rather than with fear or disgust, you will begin to understand how even the most difficult life lessons have left you stronger.* What are these injured places? They include what you might have considered your faults, character defects and even your emotions. When you are able to hold those wounded aspects of yourself with gentle compassion, they are available for healing, which allows you to move forward.

Let's consider how well people function when they are in abusive situations. Do they feel strong? No. Are they willing to take risks? No. They usually shut down. Now consider the way people function when they are in nurturing situations. They feel safe and increasingly confident. They are willing to take risks. It is much the same with self-compassion. Once you treat yourself with compassion — once you are able to look at your vulnerable places without contempt, you remove the internal roadblocks on your path. You begin to step forward with much less hesitation because you expect to be accepted for yourself. More and more, with practice, you are accepted by yourself. Your process progresses with less effort because you aren't expending as much energy to resist it.

Once you begin practicing self-compassion, you are able to open many more doors to yourself than ever before. Fear, shame or distaste have kept the doors firmly shut. Compassion for the self removes the rust from the hinges and unlocks those doors. At first, it's wise to begin practicing compassion on a feeling or old belief that isn't too emotionally charged for you. Start with something easy. Begin building your compassion skills much like you would build an out-of-shape muscle. Start with light weights and short durations. Build a history of success with compassion, being gentle and accepting with yourself about many small things and feelings, until you become accustomed to the experience of accepting yourself. Only then will you feel confident digging in deeper. Interestingly enough, when you exercise, you expect strength as an outcome. You might not have been aware that inner strength is the outcome of life's lessons.

Commitment

You'll need to rely on your sense of commitment to yourself and your individual process to develop self-compassion. As I explained in chapter 3, commitment means that you will work toward growing and honoring yourself to the best of your ability no matter what. Established habits and old beliefs are hard to shake! You tend to be loyal to the people and the kinds of relationships that programmed your limiting thoughts in the first place. The old thinking has been your identity. It takes commitment to redefine yourself by sorting through old thought patterns and reactions with the goal of finding and banishing everything that is not loving. Everything within you that is not loving is counterproductive. It is damaging to you. Without firm commitment, failure is certain. Life will not congratulate you each time you accomplish something. ☺ *You learn to honor yourself.* You cannot be committed just occasionally. Life is going to send you lessons. You must make the commitment to learn from them whenever they come up. Learning life's lessons is really the only way to move forward.

Imagine deciding to have a baby. This child's life requires your commitment to nurture and support it through both the good times and the bad times. Make the same sort of commitment to yourself:

◊ To nurture and soothe,

◊ To respond quickly to upset feelings,

◊ Not to blame yourself for abilities not yet developed.

You don't blame a baby for dirty diapers. Until your child is more mature, diapers are part of parenthood. When a baby cries for attention, the timing may be inconvenient, but you give the attention needed — when it's needed. You may grumble about climbing out of bed at four in the morning when the baby is crying, but you do get up. You deserve to commit the same kind of compassionate caregiving to yourself as you would to your precious child. Notice that you already know how to be compassionate with others.

The First Step...

The first step toward developing self-compassion is learning to feel your feelings. Don't believe for an instant that feelings aren't spiritual. Emotions are human responses to life, and as such, they reveal what needs to be healed within you. Until you heal your wounded places, you can't move forward to know your true spiritual self. Knowing, healing and growing are the spiritual path. There are many, many land mines out there, and each one is capable of blowing you off your path or tempting you to seek another path to escape from who you think you are. The object of your spiritual work is you, not someone else.

You often give others exactly what you want yourself. You are considerate, generous and tender with others, but you give it all away while you languish—and accumulate resentment. Then when you notice how resentful you feel, you label yourself as a bad person. So, out of guilt, you do more kind things for others and end up with even more resentment. Sound familiar?

☺ *Try directing some of the loving gestures you have been making to others toward yourself.* If you begin receiving some of what you send others, you'll find that there really is no shortage of love. Your heart can expand to include your own well-being without strain. When you genuinely include yourself as a cherished soul to be nurtured, your resentments will dissolve. This takes time, but it is well worth the effort. Taking responsibility in this way moves you out of the place of waiting for someone else to nurture you and repeatedly being disappointed.

The Second Step...

The second step in developing self-compassion is to turn up the volume on the critical voice droning inside your head. Until you hear it consciously, you'll believe it. What it's saying usually sounds like the truth to the unaware mind. When you have thoughts like, "I can't do this," or " I'll never make it," or "Nobody loves me," all progress stops. When you believe the truth has been spoken, you stop moving forward.

Of course these thoughts aren't true today, but they may well have been true when you were four years old. At a young age, there were many things you couldn't do. And there may have been many times when you felt unlovable and unloved. That grain of truth, however buried it may be in your past, can become magnified into an unconscious absolute truth.

When it does, it stops you dead. Since your commitment is to keep going and growing, you must learn to hear this "voice" so that you can get it out of your way.

EXERCISE 5-1

How Do You Judge Your Feelings?

In a page of your journal, make two columns, one headed "OK feelings" and another headed "Not-OK feelings." The feelings you list in the Not-OK column are the ones that require your compassion and healing. Your Not-OK feelings work like the flip of a switch that heads a train off onto a new track. When your Not-OK feelings come up, you behave very differently from how you did just moments earlier. Learning to recognize the flip of the switch takes time. Learning to stay with it takes commitment. Learning to heal it takes compassion.

If you always do what you've always done, you'll always get what you've always gotten. Nobody changes out of fear; you change when you can see how you are hurting yourself. You want to treat yourself with compassion. You want to soften your stance and move your life forward.

The Third Step...

Step three in this process is to dismiss the self-critical voice within. You can begin this process by using the meditation below. Read it through several times, or tape it for yourself so you understand the intent.

Sit comfortably in a chair and breathe deeply several times to settle in. Now notice your breathing. Let it become regular and easy, until you are not controlling it. Place your attention on the edges of your nostrils and notice that the air coming in is cool while the air going out has been warmed by your lungs. Stay with noticing that for a moment. And notice it with compassion. Don't judge. Just notice and allow what is there to reveal itself to you.

Notice how your regular breathing is encouraging you to relax. Allow your muscles to soften as you breathe your awareness down inside you. Gently bring to mind the last self-critical incident you can recall. Or choose the most recurrent one. Hear that critical voice judging you and predicting your failure. Give this voice a name. There he or she is, on the job every waking minute. Such dedication! That critical presence has been with you throughout your life, originally to insure that you learned the rules and stayed out of trouble. If necessary, this aspect of you will destroy you to keep you out of trouble! It doesn't realize it's causing you problems and it really doesn't care. Now it is up to you to thank this critical aspect for its devotion to its task, and then to tell it to retire. Of course, you can keep it around as a consultant if you wish, but that calls for a commitment to allow it only as a consultant. Consider whether you really need to be monitored by that voice. Are you that prone to rule-breaking? Perhaps full retirement is best.

Create in your imagination a ceremony and a retirement gift. Make a speech expressing gratitude for a job well done and then ask the retiree where it would like to be sent for its sunset years. Perhaps a beach in Hawaii? Complete your ceremony, and with much fanfare, launch this critical aspect into oblivion. Make sure to applaud as it fades and disappears. Now visualize yourself taking a refreshing shower and changing into clean new clothes.

Notice how you feel inside. How does your head feel? Any lighter? Using awareness of your breath, gently bring yourself back to your regular state of consciousness.

If your critical voice returns uninvited in the future, remind him or her that long service deserves full retirement. Send the critic away as many times as necessary! That's commitment.

Remember, developing self-compassion takes time. It is not accomplished in a single effort. To succeed, you must practice patience with yourself and with your process. You are learning to find and honor your own your own pace and your own way of doing things.

Feelings come up to reveal places that need healing. ☙ *Healing is done layer by layer.* It is very important to remember that. Your emotional wounds were inflicted over time and so are rarely cleared with one review or even with several good cries. Patience and self-compassion are needed to create a container big enough to support your feelings, as they occur time after time, as often as needed, until you can release what needs clearing and you are left clean and infinitely freer. When you create the image of a container for your feelings, you can envision yourself gently holding each feeling for viewing. When you view your feelings in this way, you come to understand what needs to be done. Your emotional responses to situations indicate your readiness to heal a new layer. They don't mean that you are weak or inadequate.

EXERCISE 5-2

Transforming Your Feelings

When you feel upset or troubled, breathe, hold and view your feeling with compassion, and you will be able to transform it. Here's the prescription:

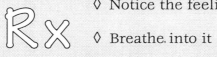

◊ Notice the feeling with compassion

◊ Breathe into it

◊ Watch it transform

Copy this exercise onto several slips of paper and post them where your eye will fall on the words frequently. Some days, you'll need a lot of reminding! Take prn (as needed).

Because you feel safe in familiar ways of doing things and because of your loyalties to old beliefs, you can expect this process to take time. When you are committed, you make time available for this cleansing process. You realize as a spiritual being that it is your life's work. It is not something you finish and then get on with being happy. If you know yourself to be a student of life, know that the clearing out and the learning are what this life is all about.

Chapter 5

Tools For Compassion

- Looking at your injured places with compassion will show you how even the most difficult life lessons can strengthen you.

- Learn to honor yourself.

- Direct toward yourself some of the loving gestures you have been making toward others.

- Learn to hear your internal critical voice so you can deprogram it.

- Healing is done layer by layer.

Willingness:
I Am Willing To Love Myself

Let go of the mind's need to have things be different.

The phrase "I am willing to love myself" is one of the most powerful agents for change I know. Nothing outside of you changes when you say these six words, but something inside does. What goes on inside is crucial because self-esteem, self-confidence and self-acceptance all come from within. You can't give those states of being to anyone else, and no one can give them to you. That's why others can genuinely love you and you may not be able to feel it, believe it, or know it. What a frustrating state of affairs! When someone sends you a message of caring, gratitude or congratulations, your inner self-assessment process is already firmly in place. You receive the message much as computers receive messages. You make sense only of the information you are programmed to receive.

Adults who grew up in houses with angry critical parents may long for acceptance, yet be "programmed" to hear only criticism. When words of genuine support and acceptance are sent your way, they are blocked by your inability to receive them. Unfortunately, children translate the insensitive ways they are treated to mean they are not lovable. They are not yet able to recognize that their parents are confused or unloving. It's important to know that the gaps your parents left in your development are the parts of your programming that will be missing when you find yourself on the receiving end of love or compassion. Love and compassion may be so inconsistent with the way you see yourself (or the world) that when you receive them, you may either burst into tears or withdraw and contract internally.

Why Is It So Hard To Love Yourself?

Loving yourself feels awkward and unnatural because you were taught not to love yourself at a very young age. I don't mean to say that most parents consciously taught their children not to love themselves. Most parents did the very best they could. But in teaching children to fit cultural norms, many parents unwittingly teach their children that they are unlovable. How could that happen? Well, it fits right into a child's natural development. As you grew, you learned that there were right and wrong ways to behave. In many cases, when you followed your natural impulses, you broke the rules of acceptable behavior. When you ran in the street, climbed the furniture, plucked rosebuds from the bush, threw stones, or ate dirt… you were constantly being told you were wrong. And you naturally interpreted the wrongness of your behavior as something being wrong with you. Of course, children must be taught the rules of safety and acceptable behavior, but if there's not enough counterbalance of loving and approval, then children are programmed to look for the rules, anticipate being made wrong, and feel defeated before they've even started. So when love comes in, perhaps in the form of a teacher who is very fond of the child, the child often responds with embarrassment and shame. He already feels that something is wrong with him, and since he is defective, he can't possibly truly be lovable. He thinks, "If she really knew me…"

Children are born egocentric, which means they believe that they are the center of the universe. If they cry, lights go on, people run in and diapers get changed. They don't know where their skin ends and mama's skin begins. That egocentrism leads to what we call magical thinking. In magical thinking, young children believe that when they think something, they make it happen. If the child wishes the parents would stop fighting, and they get a divorce, the child feels responsible for the divorce. You cannot reason with a child that it was not her fault because in her magical thoughts, the divorce happened because she wanted it to. She wanted quiet in the house and now there's a divorce and it's quiet in the house. Because she believes she has done great harm by wanting something, she learns to fear her own desires, to stop attending to them, and to stop wanting altogether.

Children also learn to feel unlovable in response to the signals they pick up from their parents. Parents who are overburdened or exhausted may not be thrilled to see their child return from school at the end of the day. The child believes something is wrong with him, not the parent. In more dysfunctional families, children are blamed outright for many family problems. "You make me tired. You're always in the way. It was so peaceful until you were born. Clumsy! Stupid!" Children believe what they are told about themselves. And who could love such a stupid, clumsy, wild child? No parent could cherish such a defective creature, they think.

Swiss psychoanalyst Alice Miller writes at great length about child-rearing in the 1930's, 1940's and 1950's. Children of that era were considered property. They were seen as unbridled savages whose spirits must be broken or they would run wild through the streets and bring great shame to their parents. So parents worked very hard not to show softness and tenderness. For example, I know that in my infancy I was placed in a crib and prop-fed. The bottle was propped on a rolled-up towel. I was not held or cuddled and I was not nursed, because of the fashion of the time. In those days many parents did not respond to children when they cried at night for fear of spoiling them. Babies were left to learn somehow to soothe themselves. As a therapist, I have met many clients in their 40's and 50's who never did learn to soothe themselves. Instead, they seek external comfort from alcohol, food, shopping and drugs.

Looking Beyond Your Limitations

Imagine an electrical outlet. You can plug in a lamp and get light — except when the flow is blocked. Have you ever seen those caps that baby-proof wall outlets? With one of those in place, nothing can get in, even though a powerful source of electricity lies just behind the cap. You can't even plug the lamp in to see if it works. If you perceive that the lamp is faulty, you stop looking before you see that the receptacle is blocked. People are like that. They only see what they've been trained to see, rendering the truth about themselves unreachable.

That sense of limitation is a real hindrance to spiritual work. There is a loving and lovable person behind those blocked receptors. Your job is to find and remove the blocks that keep you from receiving what is rightfully yours. You can't truly be on a spiritual path if you can't receive love and guidance from Divine Spirit. If your tee shirt says "God doesn't make junk (but in my case He made a mistake)," you don't believe you are worthy of love. And if you don't believe you are worthy of love, how can you make a commitment to walk the path to God and enlightenment?

Learning To Practice Self-Love

The only way to do this is

◊ To love yourself first,

◊ To see yourself as having value and purpose, and

◊ To accept that your life has meaning — as much as everyone else!

Love yourself first. Because even if you are able to accept that others regard you highly, their love can't penetrate the powerful shield of your early programming. The emptiness you experience inside will remain unfilled. Other people cannot fill your emptiness. Material goods, jobs and accolades cannot fill it, either. Only you can do it, and you must do it from the inside out.

Self-love is about coming to know yourself as a beloved child of God who is a student on the path of life. It is about learning what is yours to learn, while letting others learn the lessons that are theirs, and trusting your process.

Advancing to this level of awareness requires letting go. ☺ *As you release old ways of thinking and believing, you create space for new awareness.* And if you ask, Spirit will help you with this process. If you chant, "I love myself and I accept myself," the critic, the judge, and the prejudiced parent in your head will ridicule you and cause you enormous suffering – mostly because you've been taught that self-love is selfish, egotistical and even hurtful to others. To get around these land mines lurking in your fear mind, you can say, "I am willing to love myself." This willingness invites Divine Spirit in and initiates the process. Remember, you have no idea what you need to do to begin loving yourself. You've never done it before. Unaided, your approach might be to keep an eye on the goal of self-loving and then to whip yourself into compliance. This is why it's so important first to release old attitudes and ways of thinking. You begin this by being willing.

EXERCISE 6-1

Empty Bowl

Get yourself a bowl that you find attractive. It can be any size. Place this bowl by your bed or on your altar (place of spiritual quietude). The bowl represents you. All your beauty shows when you are empty of the problems and emotions of the day.

Each night before you retire, place the accumulation of your day's business, emotions, unsolved problems and the like into this bowl. Now you can go to sleep "empty." In the morning, after a refreshing sleep, you will find the bowl empty once again, clean and ready for the day.

Find Someone Safe

You can begin rediscovering and learning to love your genuine self by practicing with someone who feels really safe for you. Pick one person in your world, whether it's your mother or a child or a neighbor or a spouse. Make yourself a promise, that from now on, you will be totally honest with that person. Just that one person. You'll notice that when you're honest with her, she doesn't hate you; she doesn't disappear. In fact, she might even like you more because she knows who you *really* are instead of the fakey, smiling person she thought she knew. Once you've had a history of success with someone who is not threatening, you can add one more person to your list. As you feel safer and safer being your genuine self and you begin seeing how okay it really is to reveal your truth, you will begin to know, respect and even love yourself.

Suppose everyone was truthful about their desires and opinions. You would get to know who you wanted to spend time with and who you didn't want to be with. You would open yourself to being honestly respected by the people close to you and left alone by those who didn't. Doesn't sound so bad, does it?

Being Honest And Risking Rejection

Think about the games people play when they're dating. First dates are the ones where everyone is usually on their best (fake) behavior. But when it really comes down to it, why would you want to spend time with someone who's faking how he feels? And, if rejection is going to happen, wouldn't you prefer it be on the first date rather than two years, or three children later? So if you go on a date, try being who you are. "I don't like that kind of music. I'd like to try this kind of food. I'd rather do that. No, I don't want to have sex." Express whatever is truly you and just see what happens.

In practice, honesty tends to encourage honesty. Once you find out that you can be who you really are and people don't run screaming into the night, you'll realize that you're not as awful as you thought you were. As a result, you might feel encouraged to treat yourself with a little more respect.

Giving Yourself The Nice Things You Deserve

Notice what you like to do but you deny yourself. Perhaps time in a bath with sweet-smelling bath salts. Perhaps half an hour of exercise a day or some meditation or fresh flowers in the house. If you notice one or two things like that that you're denying yourself, start letting yourself have them. The first thing this will do is bring up that critical voice we were talking about. So listen to that voice and tell it, "I'm not hurting anyone. I'm not taking anything away from anyone by doing this. I'm doing this for me because I deserve it." ☺ *In other words, as you move out of your level of safety and into the risk, you trigger your fears.* First you get to hear them. Then you get to answer them.

Remembering That You Are A Beloved Child Of God

Have you ever considered the fact that God is big enough that He considers all of us His children? Suppose you allowed yourself all the rights, respect and honor that every other person on the planet deserves. No more, no less. Who would it hurt if you held equal claim to respect and honor?

When I was a child, I was taught to be polite to strangers and neighbors and all the people who lived outside the house. But inside the house, it was okay to be careless with the children's feelings. Are you cruel to yourself within and pleasant to people outside yourself? If you tend to be very outspoken and often find that you're hurting other people's feelings in your interactions, try noticing when other people wince. Maybe you ought to notice that you're wincing at those moments, too, and work on softening your approach.

Be willing to remind yourself that you are a deserving being simply because you are a member of the human race. You can feel equal to other people. Allowing yourself equality reminds you that you are indeed a beloved child of God. God did not teach you to be considerate and polite to everyone on the planet except for yourself. Include yourself and you will blossom.

Removing The Barriers To Self-Love

Ironically, when I invited Spirit into my process, life initially appeared to get worse. That is, long-buried and unfinished business came up and a new round of lessons was presented. But I had asked for it! If your commitment is strong, there's no backing down when life appears to get more difficult. The lessons are presented for your benefit from a source much more universal than you. Your work is to get in there and clean out old, stored-away beliefs. They block your ability to love yourself and they must be removed for you to grow. The more you resist, the longer the lessons take to learn. When you cooperate, life is life and suffering is optional. Don't suspend life until this "rough patch" is over. This is your life.

When you hold yourself with self-compassion, life goes easier and you remain more aware and supportive of yourself through the process of change and growth. Remember, life consists of course after course of lessons. Once one set of lessons is learned, you move on to the next course. This awareness keeps you more centered in your life and your spiritual path. Getting caught up in questions like "why me, why now, why this?" leads to suffering. Unanswerable questions always torture the questioner because they link directly into the fear mind cycle. ☺ *Instead, be willing to ask, "What has this come to teach me," or, "What can I learn from this?"* Questions like these are helpful. They can act as vehicles to get you through the pain. Know simply that what is happening in your life is here because your soul called it to you for the learning it contained.

Life contains so many requirements. You must eat, get enough sleep and go to work. You must pay taxes, vacuum, feed the dog, clean the cat box, grocery shop, etc. How many of these tasks do you approach with resentment or a sense of resignation? And will you also put your commitment to loving yourself in the same category with all the other requirements? Imagine saying, "Okay, I'll love myself, but I'm not gonna like it!" This is why willingness is so essential. Before you can love yourself, you have to work on your willingness. First things first. Trust the Divine Spirit to know the way. ☺ *Get your eyes off the goal and onto this moment.* You are spending your entire life doing your soul's work. It isn't like creating a business plan or designing a car, where all steps are accomplished with an eye on the finished product. As a human being growing a soul, you are always an unfinished product. You cannot dictate to God how you will turn out. You cannot know where you'll be in the future. It is beyond human knowing. It is the realm of the Divine. So learn to do your spiritual work and know that the overall plan is growth. You can decide to become a committed, willing, patient learner, trusting that the plan is much bigger than you alone. You can even be willing to learn that God's plan for you is far bigger and far more abundant than all the things you've been praying for all these years.

EXERCISE 6-2

Practicing Self-Love

Say the following affirmation twelve times each day, regardless of whether you believe it. Say it every time you hear yourself having unloving thoughts about yourself. Continue this exercise for 30 days and notice the changes it brings in the way you perceive life.

☺ *"I am willing to love myself."*

Letting God Take Care Of The Divine Plan

*You can blame God for withholding,
or you can look at what you are holding.*

Do you pray? And if you do, do you pray from a feeling of emptiness and lack? When that's the case, there is an element of trying to control the process. "Here's what I need," you pray. When God hears your prayer and sets the process in motion to move you toward your desire, the result may not be what you expected. Then your control response sets in. "No, no," you shout. "That's not what I asked for!" What you see immediately may not be the precise thing you're seeking, but you can trust that it is the first step in preparing you to receive what you asked for. God isn't like a Sears Catalogue, delivering answers to prayers in precise sizes or colors.

If you pray for prosperity, you're giving God permission to help you look at all the ways you're blocking the flow of affluence and abundance in your life. If you pray, saying "I need $50,000 on this job," and suddenly you get fired from your $20,000 job, it may not occur to you that your prayers are being answered. If you see yourself as a $20,000 a year person, you can't envision yourself as a $50,000 person. You don't know how to get there, so God's going to show you. You have to trust that maybe the first step is that you're going to lose your job and the second step is that a school catalogue arrives in the mail and you "decide" to sign up. Before you know it, you've taken a course in something, completed it, and now you qualify for the job that pays $50,000. But in the meantime, you are doing many things to block your spiritual progress because you don't believe you can have prosperity.

If you don't have it, it's because you don't believe you can have it.

The answer to your prayers doesn't come in one step. It doesn't come instantly. It's a progression of steps moving toward it, and clearing out all the blocks you've created to prevent it from developing.

What if your hands were full of pebbles and you prayed for a bicycle? God knows you can't ride a bicycle clutching two fistfuls of pebbles, so He doesn't deliver the bike. Instead, He sends you messages about dropping those pebbles. Nothing can come into closed hands, a closed mind, or a closed life. There's no room. Once you drop the pebbles, you make room for the bike. When the bike you prayed for doesn't show up immediately, you can blame God for withholding — or you can look at what you are holding.

Willingness creates space. It doesn't close off growth or demand quick answers. Willingness is a softening, an opening. It allows something new to happen. It helps you realize that your limited way of thinking doesn't reap the desired rewards. Willingness opens the door to the new. Use willingness to open yourself to love, patience, non-judgment and all the steps on the spiritual path.

EXERCISE 6-3

Choosing Not To Suffer

Take your time with this meditation. Its purpose is to help you notice and release.

To begin:

Settle comfortably into a chair. Breathe deeply a few times to become fully present. Now breathe normally and easily, down into the center of your being. As you do so, concerns of many kinds will crowd in, calling you back into your head. Begin packaging these clamoring thoughts, neatly storing each in its own box. Notice the nature of the thought in each box. If it is an emotional worry, place it in a pile to the left of your chair. If it is a logical concern, place in a pile to the right. Leave the boxes in their piles for a few moments as you complete the exercise. They won't go anywhere.

Notice how you feel at this point. Breathe into the feeling. Do you feel lighter? Freer? As you breathe into it, let the feeling expand through your entire body. Stay with the feeling as long as you like. Now, imagine that a vortex — a large energy vacuum — has appeared in your ceiling. One by one, toss the packages you no longer wish to keep into the center of the room. There, the vortex draws them up and transforms them into the Light. Look at the packages remaining alongside your chair. Place those that you want to hold onto back into your head. Without judgment, notice which ones you are willing to release and which you need to keep.

Say "thank you." Bring yourself back into your regular state of consciousness.

Chapter 6

Tools For Willingness

❦   As you release old ways of thinking and believing, you create space for new awareness.

❦   As you move out of your current level of safety and into the risk, you trigger your fears and then get to answer them.

❦   Ask, "What has this come to teach me?" or "What can I learn from this?"

❦   Get your eyes off the goal and onto the moment.

❦   Practice saying and feeling, "I am willing to love myself."

7

Faith:
What Is It and
How Do I Get Some?

Imagine jumping into a fast-moving river. Fear sets in as the water swirls you about, tugging and battering you against rocks jutting up in front of you. The current pulls you toward a gnarled root emerging from the river bank and somehow you manage to grab it. You hang on for dear life. The current is strong, and bits of rock and branch bruise you, but when you use all your strength, you can hold on. You're hurting, but at least you feel safe. Much the same dynamic happens on a spiritual plane when you believe you'll be safe as long as you stay where you are. You may feel safe clinging to the status quo, but you surely can't be comfortable (and the scenery never changes!).

Imagine letting go of the root, allowing the river to carry you where it's going. Not knowing where you are heading, you go in faith, with the future unknown. You decide to handle *whatever* appears, as you go with the current, floating on your back with legs ahead of you, your arms steering you clear of most obstacles as they appear. As you repel off rocks and submerged trees with your feet, you take your power back. You learn how to move more efficiently with every current and eddy you navigate. You are in the flow. It is the same with spiritual flow. If you go in faith, and keep your eyes, heart and mind open, you will learn from your journey. You will grow to handle whatever appears.

Did you know that change is all there is? Even as you read these words, different thoughts pass through your mind, your system metabolizes foods into glucose, and cells die and are replaced in every part of your body. You cannot really hold onto an instant for longer than it lasts, but fear creates the illusion of holding on. When you feel you have "stopped time" by clinging to an instant, you prolong and replay it in your mind. Instead, consider experiencing the moment and choosing to flow past it, or letting it flow past you. It is your choice. Fear demands that you hold on. Faith encourages you to let go and move along. Faith empowers you to grow.

Letting go is no easy task for most people. Holding on to difficult life experiences can be a deeply ingrained habit. People often hold on to their painful experiences because they have made such a powerful impact on their lives. They wouldn't be who they are if they hadn't had such hard times as children, or if their husbands hadn't been alcoholics, or if they hadn't endured the loss of a sibling or a child. Life events are painful and they do make an impact, but once you've learned what you need from them, you don't have to keep them so close to your heart, and you don't have to let *them* dictate who you are as a human being. You can choose not to identify yourself as a victim. You don't have to think of yourself as hopeless and helpless. Holding onto painful events enlarges and empowers them, making your pain more intense.

Letting go requires faith. (You knew there was a catch to this, didn't you?) Faith assures you that you don't need to limit your definition of yourself to the pain you've suffered. You are much more than your painful experiences! Faith assures you that you'll be safe if you let go of old wounds. *It promises that old pain won't be replaced by greater pain.* This is important. Most holding on is done out of fear that the "devil you know is better than the devil that you don't know." In other words, you're afraid to let go of what you have because you believe what comes to replace it will be worse. However, you can't have faith until you let go. You can't let go until you have faith.

The problem is that pain doesn't go away unless you choose to face it. Anything you've buried with the intention to ignore eventually turns up again because, as happens with everyone, you bury your past alive. It hasn't truly been laid to rest. The pain reappears years later as illness, divorce, job loss, phobia, etc. When you suffer physical pain, you interpret it as something gone wrong in your body. On the contrary, something has gone right. Your physical pain is trying to get your attention. As long as you are numb, you cannot grow. ☺ *When you see pain as a wake up call, you can use it to motivate your growth.* Let the pain direct you to what's up.

When buried pain builds up to the point where it feels overwhelming, most people try to numb it or retreat from it. When the pain intensifies, your mind seeks someone to hold responsible for the situation. It usually blames you. "It all happened because you moved forward, trusting something better would come."

Some people let pain stop their spiritual progress. They become sufferers. They see no options. To let go of these lessons (in the form of pain), they must realize that they are identifying with suffering.

Do you speak of "my handicap," "my illness," "my bad luck?" If you do, you can choose to release ownership of these conditions by using them as tools for learning rather than restraints preventing your progress.

Helping You Let Go

When you release a painful belief from your system, you create room for yourself. Something new will fill that space. It may not happen quickly; you may be left feeling a bit awkward and "empty" for a while, but something new will fill it. ☯ *You can ease this pain-releasing process by not trying to predict or define what will fill the void, and by not believing fear when it whispers that "empty" is bad.*

You may not realize just how much fear and judgment block your progress. When you consider letting go of an old belief, fear automatically warns, "It's not okay to let go of the old, the old has value. If you let go, what if nothing comes in? What if something worse comes in?"

Fear predicts the worst. Judgment backs fear by shaming you for feeling empty, just the way it shames you for sitting in silence and enjoying the quiet for a time. Judgment informs you that if you're going to open the door and let something out, you have to tell God what you want to come in to replace it. People often attend classes to create proper, precise affirmations. They learn to tell God exactly what they need, as if their will for themselves could be more carefully thought out or more perfect than God's will for them. When life doesn't unfold exactly the way these people demand, they begin to believe their prayers aren't answered, or that it's their lot not to be rewarded and blessed.

Prayers are always answered, but frequently not in ways you might expect. Rather than having your desire fulfilled instantly, (What would you learn from that?), you probably will receive the first in a sequence of steps toward the answer to your prayer. ☯ *To progress, you need to notice something going on in your life that's no longer loving and productive for you and decide to release it.* You release it and create a void, trusting that what comes next may not be the immediate manifestation of your ultimate desire, but the next step in your growth leading toward what you want.

For example, perhaps you ask God to give you the courage to face a personal crisis. To make way for courage, you've got to let go of the fear! So you may find that fear comes up for you. That's not what you asked for! But it's your job to clear out the fear. God offers you the opportunities to notice where fear is keeping you stuck, keeping you from locating your courage. It's like a computer's memory. You need to clean out the old files to make room for the new ones. Luckily, computers don't refuse to "let go" of the old files until they're convinced they'll like the new ones!

Interestingly enough, when you've gone through the process consciously and cleaned out the fear, you will find that you now possess courage. It's like watching a rose open. Don't pay so much attention to the individual petals, or worry about how quickly it opens. Just know that the reward is at the center of the flower. That's what will ultimately be revealed. So if you feel surrounded by fear, know that you have the nugget of courage within you. It's a matter of letting go of the petals of fear so that you can reveal the courage. It's not that God gives you the courage; it's already within you. God gives you exactly what you need to reveal your Self to yourself.

It is important to stay aware on your path, so that you can notice what's happening and fit that into the framework of what you asked for in prayer. "Aha! All the fear I'm feeling has risen to the surface so I can release it." Anyone unaware of this process would be terrified by feeling so frightened after specifically praying for courage. You've got to let go of fear before the courage can come. Doesn't spiritual growth feel cleaner and less chaotic from this perspective?

In much the same way, if you pray for clarity, you will likely be presented first with confusion. If you ask for love, you may feel intense anger or loneliness at first. Then it's up to you to decide whether the people close to you are acting in a loving way. Is it that you're not receptive to the love that's there, or is it that they're not giving it? Until you ask about love, you're not going to understand that connection. You're going to continue feeling hopeless and helpless, battered by the river. You have the capacity to find the answers within yourself. Your work is to reveal it. God will give you all the support you need in that search — if you ask.

EXERCISE 7-1

You Are More Than The Pain You Feel

Pain is like a healing crisis drawing your attention inward. This exercise is designed to help you trust that you can experience your painful feelings without fearing that pain is all there is.

Place your attention gently on something that's causing you pain. Focus on the physical sensation of discomfort or emotion that comes up. Notice what is there to discover. You don't have to react to the sensation, just breathe into it. Notice your inner processes...

Judgment

Memories

Escape plans

Exhaustion

Feelings

Thoughts.

These offer you a clearer picture of what has been stopping your growth. Noticing without judgment is the key. Notice the judging without shaming yourself for it. Notice how just noticing changes your sensations. You can't maintain intense pain or emotion for very long without a great deal of effort. Breathe into the sensation and it will transform.

Relearning Trust

You can take the concepts you are learning in this guidebook on trust until you have experienced the reality of it enough to move from believing it is true to knowing it is true. You will process the information through your own inner knowing. Does each piece fit for you? If trusting is difficult for you, it is probably because you allow cues from the outer world to define reality for your inner world. In doing this, you disavow yourself and set others up as your authorities. You allow others to define who you are. You lose touch with yourself. When you are around other people, you may focus on how you appear to them, rather than on being yourself. When this happens, you don't see or remember who you are meeting. Have you forgotten a person's name immediately after you've been intro-duced? Me, too!

Newborn infants are helpless, dependent on and trusting of their caretakers. They learn quickly whether or not their needs will be met. If they aren't met, their innate sense of trust begins to erode. If getting their needs met is paired with their value as humans (such as being fed only when they sit quietly), they learn to focus outward to establish how well they are doing. "Am I acceptable to you?" they seem to ask.

If your trust was betrayed when you were a child, you naturally have a hard time trusting now. But unless you heal your sense of trust through becoming an aware adult, you will continue interpreting life through the eyes of that wounded child. You will continue to seek permission and approval from others.

Trust can grow only with consciousness. You will need to practice having the experience of being with people who are not interested in hurting you. As you begin creating a history of safe experiences, your faith will grow. You'll learn that safety is the norm, that most people in everyday situations are really not out to get you. You'll also need to stay aware enough to notice when a situation or person is not safe. By doing so, you are empowering yourself.

Since you can't predict what lessons will come your way, you need to be able to rely on yourself, to trust your handling and interpretation of your life as it happens. And trust builds upon itself. Each event leads to further successes and enhanced understanding. You will also notice less need to manage the lives of others. The sense of accomplishment you feel from running your own life helps you back off and let others find their own ways of feeling successful.

When faith vanishes and you suddenly find your wounded child self in control again, your mind will fill with fearful predictions of disaster. Yet once you have experienced even a glimmer of peace within, you will no longer accept being ruled by the child self and you'll want to work through the fear. You can eliminate fear reactions each time you choose.

Fear is an indication that you have gone unconscious.

As a student of soul development, ☺ *you can remind yourself that other responses are available, you have choices.* Life offers unlimited repetitions of the same experiences (life lessons). As you refine your soul, you will require fewer replays of each experience to notice the emotion, understand and heal. The lessons offer opportunities to heal aspects of yourself. That is what you have asked for and why lessons are sent.

The healing process goes like this:

> When you feel "done to" by life...
>
> your feeling of victimization increases...
>
> but since you've become conscious...
>
> it no longer feels natural to be a victim,
>
> so you're spurred into action.

The action called for in this case is to slow down and notice what just happened. Ask yourself if the experience is familiar, if it is perhaps a lesson. Don't let your mind respond. This a job for your higher self. When you arrive at an answer, don't embrace it as truth immediately. Truth is experienced with a deep knowing, a felt "yes!" It comes cleanly, no judgment or shame attached.

For example, suppose you're talking to someone on the phone who suddenly hangs up on you. You notice your feelings are hurt. You can replay all the times you were abandoned by people or, you can notice that part of yourself that still needs your attention. Are you willing to release that part in this moment by honoring it and allowing it to transform? Are you willing to love yourself in a special way and know that you will never abandon yourself? That is how to heal, by doing the same thing over and over again. A thought or emotion comes up, you look at it, heal it and release it.

It is easier to look back on an event or relationship to see how this works. ☺ *Develop hindsight as a foundation for developing insight.* Explore how you came through a difficult experience and what it taught you. What was the event trying to tell you about yourself? As you practice this way of thinking, self-trust will grow. Your intention to be more trusting of your ability to live your life consciously sets the wheels in motion.

Look at the content of your Heart to learn where you are spiritually. The material contents of your life are of the outer world, and are not an accurate measurement of who you are. Did you know that the situations and relationships in your life look most chaotic when your soul is growing most? Crisis is necessary to draw your attention to whatever is ready to be healed. People attend to wounds, not to joy. Joy is one reward for refining and healing the wounded places. As you grow, you'll attend more to joy and strive to move toward it. But mostly you move away from discomfort, especially in the earlier stages of your journey.

Life is. Your interpretations don't change it. Interpretations only change how you perceive life, how you feel about life. ☺ *You grow toward faith by altering your perceptions of life.* This is a difficult, but essential task. Have you seen the bumper sticker that reads "Life Happens?" It does. It's not personal. Life is. It's how you interpret events that makes the difference.

Life is impersonal in that it's happening to everybody. It's not out to get anyone. Some people who appear to have very difficult lives may not interpret them that way. Mother Theresa, for example, who lives in poverty and holds lepers as they die, doesn't think of her life as difficult.

Consider people who have babies with profound chronic medical conditions. Even within that situation there are choices. Some people would put the child in an institution, some would keep the child at home, while others would hire someone to come in and care for her. Some people would be torn up with guilt and remorse and feel they'd done something wrong to create the situation. Others would be resentful of the burden this child is to them. And some would be grateful for the opportunity to love. It's all in their interpretation. Interpretations can be changed when situations are seen with compassion.

It's your interaction with life that's difficult or not, depending on how you react. You either deal with life or you don't. You either feel abused by it or you don't. Your reaction doesn't change life. It does change how you perceive your ability to cope with what comes along. The more you see life as impersonal and as something that's coming to you to teach you about yourself to grow your soul, the more you go on faith and realize that there is a purpose behind all this. It's not really chaotic. It's directed for each of us individually because the lessons that come to each one of us are exactly what each one needs. That's the only way in which life lessons are personal; they are definitely individualized, and so are the responses!

What harm is there in placing your faith, your trust, in yourself? You have the power to monitor your inner workings and you are far more attuned to your needs than anyone else can be. Faith in yourself is faith in something more than faith in you as a person. It is your connection with the Divine. It is the conduit through which God speaks to you of His plans for your well-being. Even when people and situations in the outer world fail you, faith within can sustain you. Eventually, your higher self can be your first resource rather than your last resort!

If a person disappoints you, don't blame God. Instead, learn to see the person as playing a role to teach you about yourself and your responses. The Universe is designed to offer you the roles you require for your soul's development, and you decide how to play them. You have called this person to you as your teacher. You can end the relationship whenever you choose. When you understand the lesson, no more teachers will be sent to help you with that aspect of yourself. Other lessons will unfold. You can trust that this is how you grow.

Finding Faith

EXERCISE 7-2

Remembering The Divine

Look over your personal history and notice what came into your life just when you needed it. Who were the hard teachers and who were the gentle ones? Who were the guardian angels disguised as people? Notice how your path has been guided so far. All of it was done through the communication between your higher self and the Divine. God has always provided what you asked for and He will always do so.

Remember that the sun is always shining above the clouds of despair, awaiting the moment you open your spiritual eyes and see.

To feel closer to God, to your higher self, go within into the silence. Here you will find the answers you seek. Go below the noise of your fearful mind. God is an ever-faithful presence in your life—full of faith in you. Feel the power of that faith. Feel His love. Notice that when you allow yourself this feeling, how much faith you feel in God. That is the conduit between you. Channels are now open for communication with Spirit. Ask your questions, seek comfort, and feel comfort being delivered. That is faith. You feel it with your being. It is not a deliberate, thoughtful act. It is a felt experience. It comes as knowing. Unseen yet powerful, felt at a level too profound for words, you are connected with the Divine.

Chapter 7
Tools For Faith

☙   See pain as a wake-up call and use it to motivate your growth.

☙   Ease the pain-releasing process by not trying to predict or define what will fill the void.

☙   Notice something in your life that is no longer loving or productive, and decide to release it.

☙   In any situation, remind yourself that other responses are available.

☙   Develop hindsight as a foundation for developing insight.

☙   Grow toward faith by altering your perceptions of life.

Patience vs. Control

All prayers are heard and answered,
but not always in the form you requested.

In today's deadline-driven world, we are apt to say, "God grant me patience... now !" Our culture pushes us to hurry, to be the first in line, to achieve at any cost. That's fine for younger souls, but rushing is very distracting and distressing for souls who are more evolved. They desire a pace that reflects inner process. Do you find all this competition stressful? More evolved souls say, "Winning isn't everything..." Younger souls interrupt, "It's the only thing!"

When you are operating from your personal power, centered in your "flow," you automatically create and experience win/win situations. Your desire is to join with others, to be of service, not to top them or gain control. When you then achieve your goal or success, it's with a sense of peace, a sense of a natural outcome. Gone is the elation of having outrun an opponent. Does this perspective interest you? Does it speak to your heart? If it does, you're reading the right book.

Impatience is a result of a desire to control. Let's get a baseline check on where you are with all of this. Before you start, remember that if you do this exercise with compassion, there will be no judgment about the length of your list. Your goal is to locate and heal your unfinished places.

EXERCISE 8-1

Patience: Where Are You Now?

Use your journal to list the situations in your life where you find yourself feeling impatient.

When you list the kinds of things you want to control, you may come up with something like this:

> *I want to control how people behave*
>
> *I want to control traffic*
>
> *I want to control my eating habits*
>
> *I want to control everything!*

But the truth is, you're not really in control of anything. If you learn to trust your body, if you get in that centered place and get in the flow, and let go of everything else, you can do amazing things. That's how you learn patience. You can experience the desire to control much like you feel fear in your body. Irritation, frustration, pressure to rush, or anxiety about performing in a certain way are all indications of the desire to control.

EXERCISE 8-2

Listening For Impatient Thoughts

Using your answers from the previous journaling exercise, list the typical thoughts you have during each situation.

Notice how your thoughts are based on your desire for things to be different than they are and how you're trying to control your feelings of powerlessness.

These are the moments to take a breath, to go inside and comfort that fearful part of you that wants control. Remind yourself that you're not in danger, that these situations are not as serious as they may seem, that impatience or controlling thoughts are merely old habits. Releasing the need to control — and thereby learning patience — is another one of those mechanical processes of eliminating the old habits one thought at a time.

I knew someone who corrected a person's choice of a word when he didn't use that word the same way. "It's a leaflet, not a pamphlet," he'd ardently claim. He argued people down to the carpet about something as insignificant as that. Their use of the word was wrong. They were wrong. He focused on how wrong and stupid people were. And he was miserable. He could no more control the words people used than he could control the time of day. But he kept trying because he was terrified of what life might bring if it was truly out of his control.

When you have issues with control, and you try to exert control over something like how someone eats or how they pronounce a word, and they continue their behavior in spite of your efforts, you feel like a failure. Feeling like a failure is frightening. So you try harder and attempt to control even more. Acting out this need to control actually damages you. Your body suffers from high stress levels and your social life suffers because most people don't stick around controllers very long.

The Illusion Of Control

What am I saying here? That you really can't control anything? What about the rules you lay down for your children? Isn't that control? Not really. You really cannot make anyone do anything they are not willing to do. Teenagers are a particularly good example. Parents who appear to be in control have in fact created relationships in which they engage the cooperation of their teenage children. There are young people who refuse to go to school. There are others who, when driven to school, go in the front door and right on out the back. There are teens who slip out their windows at night to meet friends. You cannot be with them 24 hours a day. When you make a rule for someone and he follows it, it may seem like you are in control, but in reality, he is actually cooperating with you.

You can guide the steps of your life by being aware and by making more loving and productive choices for yourself. But you can't really control your life. Let's say you're on the corporate fast track, your marriage is going well, the bills are paid, and you're driving to work. A truck swerves across the center line toward you. You couldn't have predicted that and you couldn't control it.

When you stay as conscious as possible and make loving life choices, there's no need to control, because your choices will naturally bring loving consequences into your life.

Trying to control life is like trying to hold a handful of water.

You can hold a little bit of water and you can hold it for a little while, but you can't hold it all and you can't hold it long.

Fostering Patience

Patience is the tool that gets you back into the flow and reminds you to trust. Patience is something you exercise every time you feel yourself being off center, wanting more, wanting events to move faster, being dissatisfied with what's coming your way. Patience can be achieved in the moment. It's a moment by moment thing — it's not an "I got it once, now I have it forever" kind of thing. ☺ *When you notice that you're tightening or holding, clenching or straining, or trying to make things happen in a different way than they are happening — you can regain patience by opening your hands and taking a breath.* The breathing helps you let go of the need to be in control. It reminds you that you're not in charge, that there's something much bigger at work here. It can remind you that in the past patience has served you well, and that it is all right to continue to trust. With practice, you will refine your ability to connect with patience.

When I think about how patience works within the spiritual process, dieting comes to mind. Each day, you decline dessert, filling up on more vegetables and less meat, all with an eye to a certain weight loss. You are required to face the food desires daily. Don't you wish you could lose ten pounds in one week? Or that by refusing Sunday's dessert you could eliminate your sweet tooth? Isn't it frustrating when the scale shows a weight gain when you've been trying so hard? Dieting requires enormous patience and perseverance in the face of apparent gain, holidays and emotional triggers.

✆ *Things are always chaotic before something better comes.* Think about tearing up a yard to create a garden — what a mess! Consider how awful a cake looks in the mixing process — but the results are wonderful! You can notice how this works in your life, either journaling or getting together in a group to talk about it. You can look at your progress and your history of successes so that you can start to reassure yourself. You can tell yourself that you don't need to control situations. I love the open hands-palms up gesture that says, "I don't have to hold on to this. It's not mine."

There's a saying from the Book of Runes that expresses my feeling about control, "I will to will Thy will." In other words, my only will is to let go of it. I am not in charge. I am coming to realize more and more, through my life experience and my awakening, that what God wants for me is infinitely better than what I want for myself. Think about the amount of time you spent "designing" the perfect mate for yourself. He'd have this color hair, that color eyes; he'd be this tall, he'd weigh that much. It's not about having the perfect mate, the perfect job, or all the right stuff around you. It's not about anything like that. We are here to learn. We're not here to accumulate things or impress people, or even to accomplish anything.

We're here to learn and to grow our souls.

The more we can keep focused on that simple fact, the more we can let go of absolutely everything. ✆ *I open to my lessons and I open to my abundance. I am here and present in this life and I will accept what comes."*

When that happens — and it happens gradually by degrees — you let go layer by layer. As you peel off layer after layer from yourself, you realize that something is being released. You care, but you don't anguish. Don't get in the way of what is emerging.

Put your thumb right in front of your eyes.
What do you see?

When you hold problems so closely, they're the only things you can see. You worry the problem to death. It blots out the light. You lay awake nights trying to control what cannot be controlled. You expect solutions at 3:00 a.m. that didn't exist at 3:00 p.m. You don't have to do that anymore. Really. You can just let it go. You can put the problem out there, knowing that it is in Divine Order. If a solution is right for you, if it is the next step in your growth, it will manifest in your life. There is nothing you can do to stop what's coming and there's nothing you can do to hurry it. It will come in its own time, the right time in relation to your process.

Picture a tightly closed rosebud. You can shake it, yell at it, threaten it, and it won't open one second before it is supposed to. Your life, too, will open exactly when it is supposed to. ☙ *Learn your own pace. Learn to love and accommodate your own pace.* When you honor your own pace, other people honor it, too. The more you accept yourself, the more others accept you. You don't have to defend or explain yourself. Once you accept yourself, you feel more comfortable showing others who you are, what you're thinking, how you're feeling. People will learn from that. You don't have to tell them directly. They learn by observing.

People tend to treat you just like you treat yourself. People notice how it feels to be around you. If it feels safe and comfortable to be around you, they want more of that feeling. They may not be sure why, or even what it is that they want, but they know that they want to be around it. If they don't feel comfortable, they leave. If you don't offer the lesson they need, they leave. Or you leave.

Learning Your Lessons And Moving On

Take a look at the people closest to you: your friends, your colleagues, the family you were born into, and the family you're with now. There's so much to learn from all these teachers in your life. What beliefs have you learned from them? What ways are not productive for you, even though they're still clinging to them? As you begin to grow spiritually, you may find yourself wanting to leave behind not only the old ways and beliefs, but the people themselves.

Moving on is very hard. Our culture encourages loyalty and relationships until you are separated by death. The culture dictates that you must love your father/mother/sister/brother when in fact, it may no longer be possible or necessary. At some point in your life you may look at a blood relative and realize that if this person was not a relative, you would have nothing to do with them because they are so incompatible with you, so stuck in their way of being. Perhaps they are negative and draining emotionally, perhaps they're cruel. They're just not people you want to be around. If you realize that you no longer need the lessons they bring, it's perfectly okay, on a spiritual path, to separate from them.

There's been a lot of emphasis in the last decade or so on co-dependency and dysfunctional families. People are encouraged to do whatever it takes to make those old relationships right. That's a control issue. It's not necessary. If a relationship puts you in harm's way, if it's emotionally debilitating, or physically dangerous, or if it's so extremely unpleasant that it would cost you a lot psychically to continue it, don't continue it. End the relationship in love, not in anger. You can do this by perceiving the lesson the relationship brought you, by letting go of old thinking and behavior, and by thanking and forgiving the teacher who brought the lesson. You must clear your vision first so you can know what has been happening and what you've needed to learn.

Most people won't end a significant relationship unless they believe they've tried everything to make it right. This is especially true in the case of an aging parent. You can ask for Divine guidance in these situations. "Should I stay or go? Guide me. What am I learning here? Show me." That sets the wheels in motion. You will start seeing this person's behavior in a much clearer light. You'll be able to see why you want to sever the relationship. This way, you can get all the clarity that you need, just by asking Spirit to open your eyes to what's really going on.

If your life is clogged with too many people you call friends but who are not real friends, there may be no room for anyone else to be in your life. As you begin to grow and become more open, you can allow these people to leave. This can be very scary and feelings of abandonment may come up. But know that having nothing can be very freeing. Having nothing makes so much room for possibilities. The more you let go of, the more you go in trust and the more you learn.

Patience is essential in this process because you'll find that you will need to let go of some things many more times than you could ever imagine. Envision a white velvet sofa covered with black dog hairs. The process of letting go is a lot like removing the dog hairs from the sofa, one by one. Every time you sit down, you find a few more hairs that need removing, don't you?

After you let go of people, you will enter a waiting period, during which your trust and patience are tested. Then new people will come into your life. You'll be able to relate to them in entirely different ways because they will be at the new higher learning level with you. Notice what comes up for you during that transition period. Do you feel like you'll always be alone? That you're not good enough? That you hate being alone? You may entertain a lot of thoughts that scare you while you're alone. Then one day there will be someone or something new in your environment that feels just right and natural. Perhaps it's a higher order opportunity, a promotion, or more money.

The most amazing things can come in — if you make space. Our lessons in patience are getting us ready to let go and make space for our miracles to come in. You will get lessons in patience. How you handle them is a measure of how far you've come.

Choosing To Stay

If you choose to stay in relationships that have outlasted their usefulness, you can learn from them in new ways. You can use the time you spend with that person to gauge how far you've come in your own growth. Do you take better care of yourself emotionally when you are with them? Do you set boundaries better, do you feel less anxious or depressed after a visit? The more you learn, the more you grow. Nothing is ever wasted. You can use your time together to learn more about that person's energy, about how they operate in the world. It may not be easy, but it can be rewarding to enhance your knowledge this way.

For example, when you know a person always behaves in a certain way or holds a specific attitude, notice if you still expect them to change. If you do, you're revealing your need to control. People do not change unless they are making a specific effort to do so. Rather than allow yourself to be repeatedly surprised, angered or hurt, you can let go, allow them to be who they are and concentrate instead on how you react to their behavior. If you react with fear, anger, etc., that is your unfinished business. How will you handle it? Will you avoid the person, or let the encounter teach you what you need for yourself in those situations? ☻ Clearly, knowing how someone is and what your reaction is helps you to detach rather than getting caught up in trying to "fix" them (control them) or trying to avoid the situation.

Spiritual Learning Levels

Your personal energy changes frequently. People pick up on each other's energy. Can you recall a time that you've walked into a room and immediately sensed the tension, excitement, or fear there? That's energy. People also feel energy when it shifts. On a spiritual level, the person you've been in a relationship with has been serving as a teacher to show you some unfinished business in yourself. When you finish the business — when you learn the lesson, understand it, and heal the emotional impact of it — your energy changes.

You'll find that as that person keeps coming into your life and being whoever they are with you, your reaction is less and less charged until one day, you feel no reaction. When you feel neutral, your energy has changed. You've healed that unfinished part of yourself. The teacher senses the change in your energy; he senses that you no longer need his lesson, that he's not getting a reaction, and so it's time for him to move on.

If you want to continue interacting with this person, you might want to become *his* teacher and show him the impact that his presence has had on you or someone else. When your energy changes, you are stronger and more able to communicate to this person that he's hurt your feelings or insulted you, or that the way he's acting is not productive for you. Your clear communication can also teach him what impact his behavior has on another person. If you don't want to talk about it, or if you don't feel strong enough to speak directly to him about it, you can do an internal visualization in which you ask his Guidance to hold up a mirror to him so that he can see his behavior in the reflection.

But be advised that even if your energy changes, some people will not learn lessons from you no matter how clearly you communicate. People who are not ready to learn a lesson, won't. You may not be understood. Sometimes other people's side of the lessons aren't finished. They aren't ready to learn yet, and they won't understand you. However, just having communicated strengthens you, regardless of the response. The goal is your own energy change and your own clear communication, not the other person's understanding of what you mean. You're growing your soul, not theirs. Everyone is working on their own level of spiritual development, so the language you use may not make sense to the recipient. A good rule of thumb is if you say the same thing to someone three times, and they don't get it, you're saying it for yourself, not for them. So you listen!

Lessons In Patience And Control

You'll know that you're trying to control something if you leave an encounter with someone or some situation with an emotional feeling. If phrases like, "It didn't go my way," or "I'm annoyed," or "I'm scared" flash through your mind, you need to do some work on those feelings. Work on them by releasing the feelings every time you notice them, layer by layer. (Wouldn't it be nice if we could release something just once and be done with it?) We have lifetimes of debris to release. Count on not completing the growth of an aspect of your personality in a single try. Remember, some aspects take a lifetime to fully refine.

Focus on process, not results.

When you focus on process, you don't get caught up in control and don't invite more lessons in patience. Every individual gets to be unique. Just like that rosebud. Each is in Divine Order. All you can change in this whole world is yourself. You can change how you understand others' behavior and you can change how you support yourself in the process. You can change how you respond emotionally to what's going on.

If you adapt yourself to another person's way of being, you are not being yourself. You will not feel good about the transaction. If you bend over backward to accommodate others, you lose yourself in the process. With spiritual growth come more evolved ways of handling conflict with others. It is unnecessary to win, to overpower. Yet it is also unnecessary to accommodate all people in all situations. ☙ *As you grow to know yourself, you will be the best judge of when to assert your needs and when it truly doesn't matter.*

Just Notice...

Don't fight your impulses. If you find yourself controlling, just notice. Notice how you do it, what it feels like, and try to recall what generated your need to control. You may find that you generally expect someone to be in control of situations. It's either you or the other person. This win/lose perspective is an error in thinking that leads to many more lessons in patience. Fear mind says someone must be in charge. Ignore that whispery voice just once, and see what happens. If you aren't controlling, you free yourself up to watch what's happening. You may learn that nothing bad happens, that everyone survives and life goes on. In the process, you may learn something about yourself, the other person, and about life in general. Lessons!

Allow yourself to be curious and wonder about your lessons. Your mind will try to be logical. Dig beneath that first logical answer and you'll probably find fear. Fear generates both the impulse to control and the lessons in patience. People often use the attempt to control as a method for alleviating fear. Even though it feels like it should work, the contracting that control causes just holds the fear in.. Control seems like it should work, but in actuality, the harder you fight the fear, the stronger it gets.

You can experience fear and just be in the experience. Breathe into it and ask for support from God until the fear transforms. That's not control, that's letting go.

Have patience with your own process. You learn what you learn, how you learn it, and when you learn it. How could it be otherwise? Making yourself wrong doesn't help. ☺ *Notice what does help and do more of that. In truth, you are never finished with your growth.* Growth is the purpose of all life, so how could it be completed? You are constantly refining aspects of yourself.

Early in the refinement process, you will notice only major disturbances. Later you will become more sensitive and even the minor ripples will send you back to do more work. Refinement is like emptying a metal pail full of water. At first there's a great rush of water, then a trickle, and ultimately only drops cling around the bottom and sides. If the drops are not removed, the pail will still rust.

So patience is called for. You can either bewail the fact that you are once again "in the soup," that you are going through the old pain again, or you can know that this is how it works and move ahead.

Chapter 8

Tools For Patience vs. Control

- When you notice your impatience, open your hands and breathe.

- Things are always chaotic before something better comes.

- Open to your lessons and to your abundance. Be present in this life and accept what comes.

- Learn your own pace.

- Knowing how someone behaves helps you detach rather than trying to fix, control or avoid them.

- As you come to know yourself, you'll be the best judge of when to assert your needs and when it doesn't matter.

- Notice what does help and do more of that.

Judgment: My Way or The Highway

You have been raised to fear Judgment Day.
And yet, as most of you live your lives, every day is judgment day.

Making judgments is a natural human function that begins soon after birth. Infants experience events, record information about them, and make judgments. Hot water hurts, warm water soothes, applesauce is sweet and smooth, my parents love me, my world is unsafe. As we age, the judgments we accumulate help form the basis of our future decisions.

Many judgments are molded by social norms. In some societies, for example, toddlers learn that they are members of an extended family, that they will be nurtured and protected by aunts, uncles, cousins, grandparents, and neighbors alike. The same children may learn that although everyone in their village or tribe is family, anyone else is different and is to be considered a threat. They learn to feel safe with people whose customs and appearance are familiar to them.

In the same way, as young children in our society, we learn who to trust and how to behave based on the way we are raised. If our parents demonstrate that "no one outside the family is as good as we are," then we learn to measure everyone else according to our family norms. In this situation, our "tribe" is extremely limited. Very few people fit our requirements for being acceptable. We may extend acceptance to everyone who lives in our neighborhood, or attends our church, or speaks our language. But anyone else is different, and different is wrong, different is unsafe, different is "not us." These are the kinds of judgments that keep us feeling isolated in a world populated by billions of people. These feelings also separate us from God.

In order to evolve spiritually, we need to discover how to unlearn or let go of the kinds of judgments that keep us feeling isolated. As we let go of judgments, we begin to interpret differently what's going on around us. Our emotional responses gradually shift from intensity to detachment. The social and cultural differences that once defined us begin to dissolve, and we move toward a feeling of closeness or even oneness with other human beings on the planet. And we can experience a connection with the Divine.

As we progress through clearing out old, unnecessary judgments, we broaden our definition of family to include everyone. We move toward the realization that on a spiritual level we are truly one family.

The way we interpret the events and people we encounter indicates where we are spiritually. As we are able to release our negative "not us" interpretations, recognizing that every person is precisely where he or she should be on the spiritual path, we make room in ourselves to absorb more of life with a spiritual understanding.

How Does Judgment Slow Your Progress?

The easiest way to observe your own judgments is first to notice when other people are making judgments. Listen to social conversations about "them versus us," or about "that person's behavior versus my way of doing things." Then begin to notice your own behavior and reactions. Do you join those conversations? Are you repelled by those conversations? Do you, when you're alone with your own thoughts, judge people or institutions? Eventually, you'll be able to notice your self-judgments. Those are the hardest to notice, mostly because they're so constant. They're like patterns on the wallpaper or part of the scenery.

Keep in mind that when you are judging others, you are judging your-self, because in truth, we are all connected spiritually. The spiritual process is not about everybody out there, it's about the self. So when you judge another person even in a small way, your self knows that and it hurts you. There's a saying often used in 12-Step programs, "When you point a finger at someone else, three fingers are pointing back at you." Judgment is point-ing a finger.

Spiritual development moves us forward. Judgment shuts everything down. It's like turning off a machine. If you're judging somebody, you're not interested in learning anything more about them. You don't care about their reasons for doing what they did, or how they understand their world. You're just pronouncing, "Bad!" or conversely, "Good!" Both mean you don't have to explore any further. But if you witness a woman yelling at her child and, rather than judging her, you say to yourself, "That mother is looking stressed and is taking it out on her child," you've opened yourself to understanding more about the mom and her interaction with the child. You have opened yourself to more possibilities than fear and a need to control would allow.

EXERCISE 9-1

Noticing How You Judge Others

Take a few minutes to list what bothers you about habits, groups of people, afflictions, political or religious affiliations, behaviors (remember war, cruelties, uncleanliness, small annoyances, overeating, etc.) Be honest, but be kind about how you evaluate yourself once you complete your list. These things are where your judgments keep you stuck. Your list serves to let you know what's available to work on. Remember, everyone makes judgments.

Noticing Self-Judgment

You can look at how you judge other people, but ultimately you need to look at how you judge yourself. With self-judgment, you keep yourself isolated by believing that you are the one who is bad and different, that you are unworthy, ugly or stupid. Self-judgment paralyzes you. It defeats you. It causes immense pain and despair.

When you start noticing how much you judge yourself, you realize that the enemy is within. You can never escape from yourself. You can go out in public and put on a smiling face and do good works and people can think you're wonderful, but if your self-judgment says you're a fraud, or didn't do enough, then there's no relief. There's nowhere to turn. There are no choices. There's just, "I'm bad. Whatever I do is bad. Why should I try anything new?" Why would you want to try something else, why would you want to exercise options or take risks in personal growth if you've come to know that you're going to get smacked by your self-judgment every time you try something?

The following exercises encourage you to explore what you have to work on within your personal spiritual process. Be careful not to judge yourself harshly about where you are on the journey. You are precisely where you are supposed to be. Remember, it is your choice to hold onto judgments (and remain where you are spiritually) or to release judgments (and advance to higher levels). You cannot release before you are ready. Pretending to release won't accomplish anything but frustration and guilt. On the spiritual path, you can't lie to yourself because you can't hide from God.

Until you *notice* the judgments you make, you cannot begin to heal them. Let's begin this exploration with noticing self-judgments.

EXERCISE 9-2

Noticing Self-Judgments

List all the ways you are aware of judging yourself. Remember, you can't heal them if you can't acknowledge them. You might start by asking yourself what you don't like about yourself. Often self-judging statements begin with "I am too..." or "I am less than..."

Please keep in mind that even though you might not feel proud of what you've written down, you have to reveal your judgments to heal them. They are like hooks laying in wait to snag you into unloving and isolating thoughts.

Judgment's Impact On The Self

Now, let's go even deeper. Take the time to carry a small pad and pen everywhere with you for one week. In it, write down all the judgmental thoughts that enter your mind, recording as many as you can catch. Notice them while eating, bathing, driving, etc. (If your inner judge is anything like mine, you may need a tape recorder because you can't write as fast as you think!)

After the week has ended and you've recorded those negative thoughts, you can begin the next step. On a fresh sheet of paper, make two columns, one of your negative thoughts about others and one of negative thoughts about yourself. Read over your "others" list for possibilities to add to your list of self-judgments. There you have it. Seven days worth of poison that's been administered to your body, mind and spirit. This is what your inner judge thinks of you and the world.

The best way to eliminate these self judgments is one thought at a time. I know, you were hoping for a clean sweep and a fresh start, but this is a mechanical process. Knowing what is there to be released is 50 percent of the battle. The sooner you get started, the sooner you'll experience the freedom that comes from creating a more spacious mind and a body that isn't being poisoned by a steady drip of negativity. You're worth the effort. One thought at a time.

Remember, you didn't create these negative thoughts overnight and you've been rehearsing them for decades, so they won't vanish overnight. Following the seven-day period, make yourself a commitment (there's that word again!) of 30 additional days to weed out, erase, send into the Light, all the negative judgmental thoughts you find in your head. See what happens. Remember, your spiritual work is your life's work, so if you need to work at clearing judgment for a much longer time, don't judge yourself for that.

EXERCISE 9-3

Releasing Judgment

It's time to create ways to support your commitment to releasing judgmental thinking. Let your imagination help you. Try the methods I've created and add your own as needed.

1) *Notice if certain moods or physical conditions — like loneliness, depression, hunger, exhaustion — are present during outbreaks of judgmental thinking. When you're feeling judgmental in these situations, it likely stems from feelings of unworthiness, loss or lack. Support your commitment by attending to your needs more regularly. Give yourself what you need and you'll be less inclined to lash out at others.*

2) *Choose things or people you often judge — like a boss or road conditions or a specific group of people — and write each on a separate slip of paper. Put all of them in a container. Each day, select one judgment to consciously release. Write reminders of the judgment on Post-It notes and stick them everywhere you go — the bathroom, the car, the office.*

   You can attend to one judgment a day, or stay with the same judgment as long as you need to let it go. Or, you might rotate through your judgments, doing one a week, one a month or one a year.

3) *Now, you create some ways to notice and release judgments. When you drift away from this releasing exercise — and you will — judgmental thoughts will call you back again and again. Be gentle with yourself and start wherever you are. The work is lighter when you don't judge yourself.*

Know Yourself, Know Humanity

In the mind of God, we are all one family. Therefore, to know yourself is to know everyone. Truly. If you know yourself, you get to know that spark of divinity within you, and then you can begin to see it in every single person you meet. The saying, "a stranger is a friend I haven't met yet" is a good expression of that realization. As you feel more confident in yourself, you may find yourself in a mall or on a crowded street, looking at strangers and smiling. Most often, they'll smile back, and perhaps say hello. They won't be frightening strangers anymore. You won't waste time wondering what's going on inside their heads. You won't need to worry about how they're judging you. You'll just be sharing a moment of being connected. It will feel very good. Both of you will have been enriched.

Judgments are comparisons. How can you know who you are without comparing yourself to others? First of all, others are not the standard. When you compare yourself to others, you are making them the standard for acceptability. Or you're making yourself the standard. If you're saying, "You're not like me, and therefore you're 'less than,' " then you are the standard by which all others should be judged. When you look at it that way, you see the arrogance in it. The arrogance is coming from low self-esteem. When you get to know yourself and see that you're an ordinary person who is a precious being, just like every one of God's children, you'll be able to see that preciousness in everyone. Then you can see everyone else as students on the spiritual path, too. This kind of recognition and acceptance is part of larger process of spiritual growth that takes time. In fact, it takes as long as it takes.

A Reminder: God Is Not Judging You

God is not judging you as you move through your process. Can you hold that thought in your consciousness? God knows the sum total of you — past, present and future — and does not judge. Imagine that. God is love. He has no other choice of behavior. He loves saint and sinner alike because He knows all people are learners who are not perfect and, as such, are not expected to be! You are not expected to be perfect. Imagine that!

The Spiritual Levels Of Judgment

Read this section without judgment, if you can. This is information about your spiritual state of health, much like taking your temperature. These spiritual levels of judgment offer information about your progress. With that information, you can make decisions. Don't limit yourself with thoughts of being "good" or "bad," just notice where you currently are.

First Level of Judgment:

◊ *Categorizing people in groups, races, cultures rather than as individuals*

◊ *Not empathizing, not attempting to understand others*

◊ *Labeling others based on a few characteristics*

◊ *Wanting to be like the oppressor, wanting to be the "strong one"*

Second Level of Judgment:

◊ *Believing in revenge and demanding retribution*

◊ *Responding with strong emotions*

◊ *Seeing a wrongdoer as his role (like killer or thief) rather than as a human being*

◊ *Feeling the victim's pain*

Third Level of Judgment:

◊ *Identifying fully with the victim in everyone*

◊ *Reacting physically, as if it was happening to you personally*

◊ *Attempting to understand the motivations of the wrongdoer*

Fourth Level of Judgment:

◊ *Understanding and accepting that suffering is part of the eternal experience*

◊ *Believing in the ongoing nature of life*

◊ *Believing in the indestructibility of the soul*

Fifth Level of Judgment:

◊ *Feeling the peace that emanates from a sense of oneness with all beings, from knowing that suffering on the physical plane also brings spiritual teaching to those who are open to learning from it*

◊ *Believing that each individual creates his or her own reality*

◊ *Noticing that a non-judgmental withdrawal from what is unevolved speaks of the many lessons you have learned*

Did you observe that in each succeeding step, the level of emotional response diminishes? 🕉 *Noticing your emotional reaction can help you gauge your development, therefore, as your emotional reaction is healed, layer by layer, the mind can let go and the soul can absorb the learning brought by each person in your life.* Holding onto emotion fills the self, clogs it up, and stops growth.

Most people function simultaneously on *several of the spiritual levels of judgment*, depending upon the situation. Some people will cheer as a boxer is knocked out (Level 2) and shudder if a horse is whipped (Level 3). Others may believe that gum chewing is a sign of weak intellect (Level 1), but would never hurt a child (beyond Level 1).

All of your responses and reactions provide information about your level of "judgmental" development. Don't confuse spiritual development with chronological age. Our bodies may mature, but our understanding of Truth may not. We don't have to remind our bodies to develop or age, but we can consciously remind ourselves to be open to spiritual development. We can choose to grow or to remain the same. So what you do with the information about your level of spiritual development is up to you. Just remember that retaining judgments prevents you from moving forward spiritually. As you mature from the emotional reactions of childhood to calmer adult responses, you reflect earned wisdom. As you age, you build a storehouse of life experiences that can enable you to make most intense emotional reactions unnecessary. For example, a baby will startle and wail in fear at the sound of a balloon popping. A 4-year-old will startle at the sound, but wail only if the balloon was a cherished possession. A 10-year-old will startle, identify the source of the sound, and go about her business. As you mature, you learn to respond to events by first checking your perception. Is there real danger here?

Growth on the spiritual path also leads you to an awareness that you wouldn't trade your life for anyone else's, and that all people are where they should be, who they should be, and doing what they need to do. With the information you received from the levels of judgment exercise, you can discover where you are and where you want to be. Now you are more aware when you think or behave in ways that reflect a closed, judgmental system toward yourself and others. ☯ *Noticing gives you choices.*

As you move consciously through these levels of judgment, you will release intense emotion in favor of wisdom. Rigid divisions of good and bad transform into life lessons beyond simple categorization. This is true freedom. Imagine being free of emotional reactivity and judgment!

Clarifying Judgment, Perception And Choice

There are important differences between judgment and perception. Judgment generalizes, "All men do..." "all conservatives think...," "those people..." Perception realistically distinguishes. Any judgment—either all bad or all good—is not accurate because humans are so complex. We all have many parts, events have many components and situations have at least two sides. If you can be perceptive rather than judgmental, you can be open to what works and what doesn't work for you. Perceptive people aren't driven by the need to fix or change others because they recognize that others are on their own paths, just where they need to be. If you don't like them, you don't have to be around them. (Or you can choose to stay and learn from them!) Each behavior, each belief, each person is distinguished as a bit of information to be understood as comfortable or uncomfortable to the self. When you know that someone else's behavior is at his or her learning level, it becomes easier for you to detach emotionally. You can release taking it personally.

As you move past making automatic judgments to discerning perceptions, you create more choice for yourself. Noticing a facet of another person that you can't tolerate actually tells you what you need to do, not what the other person needs to do. Do you want to create some distance between yourself and this person because of the characteristic? Do you want to end the relationship? Or perhaps, on balance, relationship with this person is beneficial to you and you just need to avoid a mildly troublesome topic or situation. Furthermore, letting go of judgment creates room inside of you for new relationships, new experiences, and new lessons. It also creates a space for you to look at current events with new ideas. Create space and you'll move on and grow. If you always do what you've always done, you'll always get what you've always gotten!

As you separate out your judgmental thoughts and tune in to how you feel about a person or event, you are refining your perceptions. Remember, judgment comes in the form of fearful thoughts. You want to be able to see what's really there. For instance, if someone is in danger, or if someone is being hurt and you perceive it, you can act immediately, in whatever way you choose. Making a judgment about the event means that you're proclaiming it bad and wrong when it really may not be bad and wrong for that person's learning level. It may be what they need to be doing or learning. It doesn't mean you have to let them continue doing it. You also don't have to condone it. If, for example, the person you observe hurting someone else has come into this life as an abuser and has come to learn lessons about abuse, he won't learn the lessons unless people stop him and let him know that it's unacceptable to hurt others. He needs to be punished for it by the society that calls it abuse. On a soul level, the abuser is not "bad" or "wrong," but is asking to be taught what is not acceptable on a physical level.

When you move beyond automatic judgments into perceptions and options, you feel more connected to others, because you are then connected to yourself. It's like opening all of your own circuits so that you connect with all the circuits in the people around you. You won't do this as long as you feel unsafe (as long as you feel judged), so let's find out where the judgment is coming from.

Reread this chapter until it begins to make sense to you. Do the exercises for the information they provide. Know that this is your work. Let others do theirs. Notice over time how you eliminate judgments as you become aware of these negative thoughts and as you detach from an emotional need to control yourself and others.

The more you release, the freer you feel.

Chapter 9

Tools For Judgment

☙   The most effective way to eliminate self-judgments is one thought at a time.

☙   Decreasing emotional reactions can help you gauge your development.

☙   Noticing gives you choices.

10

Anger:
Do You Want To Be Right
Or
Do You Want To Be Happy?

*The process of living is not one of organizing and controlling,
but one of living and learning.*

Do you want be right or do you want to be happy? Hear the challenge
in these words. You are being offered the opportunity to take responsibility
for repeatedly falling into anger. Whether you call it irritation, annoyance
or frustration, it is still some degree of anger. You create it by memorizing
and holding onto your lifetime of both conscious and unconscious emotional wounds. Releasing anger requires you to be able to see it in yourself
and to understand where it comes from.

Creating Anger

Imagine a boy who grows up with a father who is too busy to spend time with him. His father measures him, in passing, by grades and soccer scores. This boy grows up angry at what he perceives as abandonment or rejection by his father. Unless he finds a way to understand and release his lonely childhood experience, he will continue to find abandonment and rejection in his adult relationships. He will expect to be abandoned. That expectation will override reality, and when he actually is loved or accepted, his fear will drive him to withdraw. And the people who genuinely love him will feel rejected and ultimately abandon him. But he won't see how he created the cycle and he will be angry, "See, I'm right. This happened and I hurt. In fact, this always happens. I'm always misunderstood (or attacked or abandoned). Life stinks. I never get the love I need."

Using the words "never" and "always" are red flags warning that you are rehearsing your pain again. Children think in terms of Christmas "never" coming or Mom "always" yelling. When adults think in terms of never and always, they are feeling as powerless as children. Their anger is a response based on personal history. The fear mind is programmed to see and interpret life in a certain way, and will continue to do so until you delete all the old programming and install the new. This is your life's work.

The way to create anger is:

◊ *Event...*

◊ *Thought about the event...*

◊ *Interpretation of the event based on personal history...*

◊ *Pain resulting from the interpretation*

Interpretations create the anger. These perceptions are colored by our past experiences and how we felt about them as children. Keep in mind, children are fairly powerless and have a limited choice of options. They must submit to the power of "Because I said so," "It's for your own good," and "Do it or you'll get a spanking." Imagine the anger in a child who is allowed little or no voice in decisions regarding his body, his feelings or his life. He's sent to his room to isolate his feelings, and in that isolation he feels rejected—and angrier by the minute. And not allowed to express his anger.

All parents control their children to some degree, and in so doing, some of the children's needs go unmet. Unmet needs cause emotional wounds that vary according the level of control and the personalities of individual children. How those wounds are acknowledged and healed also depends on the child growing to adulthood. Unconsciously holding onto personal history well into adulthood is one option. Consciously realizing automatic and perhaps erroneous responses is another choice.

Try this new scenario:

    ◊ *Event...*

    ◊ *Thought about the event...*

    ◊ *Interpretation of the event based on personal history...*

    ◊ *New thought, "That kind of thinking causes me pain and pain is no longer an option."*

The man who fears abandonment could try this after once again failing to get a second date. Here's his thinking, "I can get a first date. But why won't she go out with me again? Why doesn't she like me? I am such a failure. No, she's a loser! I wouldn't date her again on a bet! Wait a minute... this is familiar. I can see that she didn't like me so I feel worthless and now I'm angry at her. Maybe I could pay better attention on my next first date. Maybe I'll choose more carefully, I'll watch how I act to see if I'm sabotaging myself somehow. I don't want to keep hurting and feeling lonely."

When Pain Is No Longer An Option

The focus in spiritual growth is not on how to change other people or life events. It is learning how to notice when you're interfering with your own happiness by rehearsing your pain. As you begin your lessons in letting go of your old way of being, you will start seeing a strong connection between a new event, your old interpretation of it, and the abrupt ending of feeling centered and peaceful. It happens in a heartbeat. It's so instantaneous that you automatically come to accept your interpretation as truth. This is what's going on when people disagree about "what just happened" in a relationship. Both have their private pain to rehearse and to do so, they need to interpret the event according to their personal scripts. They need to feel that they are right to keep the pain cycle in motion.

> *These interpersonal cogs will continue to engage and turn each other automatically until you shove a stick in to stop them. The "stick" that stops the endless circular motion is "Do I want to be right or do I want to be happy?"*

When you introduce this thought, you open things up by acknowledging that you do have options. You have the option of how to interpret the events in your life. ☺ *Your happiness actually depends more upon your interpretations than on the events themselves.*

Happiness Is An Inside Job

Once you begin to take responsibility for your happiness, you can guarantee that you'll get more of it. Because you live inside yourself, you can be the first to know when you're feeling off-balance, unhappy, or uneasy. It's likely that in the past, other people knew how you felt before you did by reading your facial expressions. Your mood, tone of voice or choice of words are automatic responses to life events. Suffering results from shifting responsibility for these automatic responses from inside to outside. When you make that shift, you also transfer responsibility for your feelings to other people. But since other people have their own sets of unconscious responses, they react to your automatic behaviors rather than trying to fix them. This is how you set yourself up for repeated situations in which you will feel abandoned, unloved, alone, etc.

EXERCISE 10-1

What Phrases Are Familiar To You?

◊   *If I have to ask for something, it doesn't count if I get it.*

◊   *If (s)he loved me, (s)he'd know what I want.*

◊   *I do so much and I ask for so little.*

List more of your familiar phrases in your journal.

Imagine that you're a working mother with several young children. You've come home late, dinner is delayed and the house is a mess. You scramble to catch up, while the children, picking up on your tension, become cranky and demanding. You've about had it with taking so much responsibility around the house, but you don't delegate any chores, you just fume about having to do all this alone. Your husband comes home after a difficult day with his colleagues. You expect some help managing the house and family; when you don't get it, you feel cheated. Although you haven't asked for any help, you think, "He never helps me. He just doesn't understand how hard this is for me!" Your husband, on the other hand, expects some quiet, comfort and understanding. When he doesn't get it, he feels abandoned. He thinks, "She's always crabbing about something; she never has enough time for me." Both of you have come into the interaction feeling empty and in pain; each expecting to be fixed by the other, but you have reacted automatically and the result is disappointment and frustration.

When, as a student of spiritual growth, you learn to intervene on your automatic responses, suffering becomes optional. If one person begins to change in a relationship, the relationship itself changes because automatic, knee-jerk reactions don't work anymore. Space for change has been created. But keep in mind, the goal of changing your responses is to stop the suffering in your own life. You are under no obligation to stop the suffering that others choose to experience. (And you can't stop it anyway.) Keep your focus on yourself.

Avoid stalling your growth with relationship bargains. ("I changed a little, now you change a little," or "If you don't make some changes, all bets are off!") Relationship bargains don't work. Your commitment is to yourself and your own spiritual growth. Your commitment is to continue guiding yourself toward inner peace. In that place, you don't have to be right in order to be happy. So what if you're right about being the only one in the relationship who is growing? What is your motivation for changing in the first place? Are you doing it to change someone else, or are you trying to feel peaceful and centered within your life?

Lessons In Healing

Spiritual growth is a process of reducing or healing our emotional responses to life. This is accomplished by seeing emotions as signs pointing inward to show what is out of balance within us. Life lessons stir emotions which leave us feeling off-balance, thereby stimulating our desire to heal.

When balanced, we are in a centered place within ourselves which is neither overly emotional nor coldly intellectual. The healing process is the same for everyone, but not everyone has the desire or the courage to do what's required to accomplish it.

This lesson in healing is about you. Teach it to yourself before you begin looking around for someone else you would like fix. Do this one for you. Listen to your inner dialogue to discover what your general pain-rehearsal theme is.

EXERCISE 10-2

Your Lesson In Healing

Most people have one dominant theme that creates their lessons. Can you identify yours? I often feel:

◊   *Abandoned*

◊   *Rejected*

◊   *Overpowered*

◊   *Crazy*

◊   _____

Once you have determined your basic theme, write the word on several Post-its and put them up at home, at work, and in the car to train your-self to notice when this response has been triggered. Life will generously trigger it as many times as it takes for you to see it and heal it. You really do have the choice between feeling like a perpetual victim or seeing and healing your pain.

Once you've defined your usual response (abandonment, rejection, powerlessness, etc.), follow the pain back to your interpretation of the life event that triggered it. Consider someone whose mother disciplined her with a loud angry voice. Now, as an adult, any anger or yelling, even pushiness or aggressiveness, triggers those old feelings of powerlessness. To heal the feelings, she can breathe into the fear and hear her mother's voice. She can remind herself that there is no danger in the present because now she has the power to keep herself safe.

With lots of practice, you'll learn to disassemble the cars of this train from the caboose to the engine — which represents your deepest fear. Fear is what has been driving you and your automatic interpretations. Most of us see events through the eyes of our deepest fears and feelings of power-lessness.

Once you recognize your interpretation of the triggering event, you'll be able to hear an inner dialogue that's likely to go something like this, "See, I told you so. I'll never win. Why does this person hurt me so? I try so hard. I should just give it up as a lost cause..."

Here is where your newly conscious mind can intervene. "Wait," you can say. "Remember, pain is no longer an option. Now, do I want to be right (about never winning) or do I want to be happy?"

Like all lessons in healing, this one is simple to understand and diffi-cult to accomplish. Please remember your commitment. Reread the com-mitment chapter as many times as you need. Gather your resources (books, tapes, people, counselors) around you to support your process. Although it is certainly not necessary, you may want to join or form a support group, in which like-minded members learn to listen to each other with respectful silence and complete non-judgment.

Being in a group like this can give you a blueprint for compassion. It can allow you to practice showing compassion for others as well as allow-ing yourself to receive it. If you experience a feeling of deep longing while you are in the presence of compassion, know that you are revealing a place inside that yearns for healing. Experience the longing, hold it gently, breathe into it, and watch it transform.

Be honest with yourself about how safe and comfortable you feel with a group. You are unlikely to open up if you feel unsafe. You may prefer to see a counselor individually and save leaderless or therapist-led groups for later. Once you understand and have healed some of what makes you feel unsafe, you may be ready for group work.

Remember, you are learning your own way of doing things. So much pain has been caused in the past by submerging the self to submit to someone else's point of view. That is no longer an option for students on a spiritual path. All ways are fine. Everyone gets their own and no one can impose their way on another—without permission! So become aware of when you lose yourself to please another person. Become aware if you choose to sit silently withholding your opinion and feeling the anger that accompanies your silence. How do you lose yourself in the presence of others? Are you willing to take responsibility for your life? This is how you set yourself free.

Chapter 10

Tools For Anger

- ☺ When you rehearse your pain, you automatically recreate it in any siuation.

- ☺ Old ways of thinking are causing pain and pain is no longer an option.

- ☺ Your happiness actually depends more on your interpretations of events than on the events themselves.

- ☺ Identify your usual emotional response and post it where you'll see it often to train yourself to notice when this response triggered.

11

Guilt And Fear

Take your life moment by moment rather than crisis by crisis, and see what's there.

Imagine entering a hospital room where someone is on life support. Tubes, wires and beeping monitors surround the patient. You feel drawn to this person, intensely curious about who she is and why she's there. As you peer down into her face, you realize that the patient is you. Suddenly she's in distress, gasping and struggling, clawing at the sheets. Red lights flash. Alarms sound. A nurse scurries in. She briskly checks the patient, the monitor, then sees you standing there. "Your feet," she scolds. "Look where you're standing!"

You look down to find yourself standing on your own oxygen line, denying yourself the very air you need to survive. Now, do you leap off the hose to save yourself or does guilt over yor mistake freeze you in place? As precious time passes, does your mind race, denying what's really happening, desperate to find another explanation? "Surely I can't be responsible for my suffering!"

Such inaction is an automatic response for a lot of people. They freeze up with fear and guilt over having done something wrong. For many people, breaking the rules can feel just as life-threatening as standing on the oxygen hose. For children, learning the rules is a basic survival skill. When parents harshly criticize their children for asking "stupid" questions or punish them for not knowing any better, the children become cautious. They slow down, learn indirectly, take fewer risks. Children can't know everything, and sometimes they feel they aren't free to learn and grow without risking the loss of their parents' love and support. But nature requires children to learn and grow. Thus a process that would otherwise feel natural and expansive may produce a potent conflict; children's undeniable need to learn and grow pitted against fear of their parents' disapproval and guilt over making mistakes. For example, when a child is acting her age, she may not know how to do what the adult expects. The child is not willfully resisting, she simply has yet to learn this skill. How the adult deals with this will determine how the child feels about herself.

The Origins and Standards of Guilt

Guilt is deeply entrenched because it is learned at such an early age. Standards and guilt are hard-wired into the personality, since parents socialize their children from birth.

Unless you were one of the lucky children who grew up allowed to make mistakes without ridicule, you are likely to experience some level of guilt and fear just for being your natural self. If you can look closely at guilt and redefine it for yourself, you can put it into its proper place in your life.

Guilt is a slippery companion, hard to grasp, elusive and confusing. Getting hold of guilt is like trying to pick up the ball of mercury from a broken thermometer. No matter how you approach it, it slips away and evades capture. Yet left loose, it's dangerous. Contained within the thermometer, mercury serves a valuable function. When guilt is contained within realistic boundaries, it too, serves a purpose.

Like mercury, uncontained guilt splits into countless small pieces, all rolling off in different directions. Letting guilt poison your life doesn't do you much good, does it? Your goal is to find and contain guilt so that it can serve only its appropriate purpose of keeping your behavior within accepted norms. As you learn to recognize inappropriate guilt and to regard yourself with compassion, you are learning to step off your own oxygen hose. You are discovering what is getting in the way of your healing and then removing the impediment with compassion.

If you approach the issue one guilt feeling at a time, you'll find yourself battling a many-headed dragon who simply regrows each head after it's lopped off. It's easiest to understand guilt by going to its origin. As a newborn, you were at the same time completely helpless and filled with boundless potential. You were acted upon by two forces:

1) An inner drive to learn everything you needed to survive, and...

2) Outer influences that taught you and moved you forward. At first, the two forces are about equal. But your helplessness and dependency quickly shifted greater importance to outer forces as your parents began teaching you the rules of the family and society.

When you were a baby, the outer forces around you seemed to have all the information you wanted and needed. So you adapted your needs to the judgments and the standards of those outer forces — your primary caregivers. If you were fed on a four-hour schedule, for example, you learned to wait. If your crying wasn't answered by comforting, you may have learned to withdraw in silence. Since you had no way to compare your survival lessons with rules and regulations learned by other babies and children, you naturally accepted the ways of the adults in your life. This is a normal and universal process.

Parents and institutions like churches and schools teach children what to think and feel, and for the most part, children absorb this learning as their own belief system. This process of teaching a child to live in society is called socialization. Children are taught what their group (family, church, etc.) believes in and expects of its members. There are many inconsistencies in society's lessons and children often feel confused. For example, a child is taught not to hit, but is spanked for spilling milk. Or a child is taught that "God is love" by a religious leader who sexually abuses him. Or a parent who teaches her child to be truthful lies to cover for her husband's drunkenness. Children are taught, "Do as I say, not as I do."

A typical childhood is filled with overt and subtle contradictions. Mixed messages are delivered with a raised eyebrow, a sniff, a stony silence, perhaps even a smile. How do children, these young students of life, figure it all out? First, children try to meet everyone's standards. They learn what each adult requires and try to provide it in all situations. Since adult standards are often contradictory, children frequently find themselves in circumstances where the rules say "do it" and "don't do it," real no-win situations. Now how do they succeed? Children don't have the ability to sort through snarls like these. As a result, they feel frozen by the guilt of failing someone's expectations and by their inability to sort out the confusion. When children realize that they're doing something "wrong," they feel they are bad people for doing it. Children simply don't have a perspective mature enough to realize they are not bad for failing in a no-win situation.

Children are adept at taking on guilt. If the adults around them don't take responsibility for their own mistakes, children do it for them. Children will also take on the guilt of other family members, and later in life, as adults, they take on guilt not being felt by society itself. Feeling guilty can become a way of life. It can turn compassion into fanaticism, for example, as in certain groups of political activists who harm others and themselves in an effort to help their causes.

Dismantling Guilt

Unless you are aware that chronic guilt is unhealthy for you, you are unlikely to question the basic truths of your childhood. They did fit in with all the other rules and regulations that make common sense to us, "Don't spit at people, cover your mouth when you cough, don't ask for what you want, wipe your feet when you come in from the rain, be nice at any cost, and don't push in line."

The impact of guilt-laden messages learned in childhood cause you as an adult to feel unnecessary guilt in countless situations today. If you behave from your "child understanding" of what's right and wrong, you deny yourself what you need to live as a healthy adult — your own set of ethics. Once you uncover some of the unhealthy messages you hold in your cache of unconscious rules to live by, you can begin living according to what is right and wrong according to your own standards.

You must examine and question your guilty feelings from childhood to move forward toward wholeness. Your adult mind must be in charge in this area or you will live your life as a misdirected, frightened child who is often paralyzed at the prospect of disappointing someone. Your adult self knows that you don't hurt people on purpose.

When you feel guilty, ask yourself if you are actually harming someone. Then ask yourself if you are taking responsibility for the other person's potential reactions. Once you've answered these questions, you have the power to free yourself and to let other people be responsible for themselves. For example, could your belief that life must be fair keep you from confronting a neighbor about their barking dog because your car alarm goes off occasionally?

EXERCISE 11-1

Dismantling The Guilt Response

As you become aware of your own personal "guilt buttons," record them in your journal. Allow your adult self to look them over and help you dissolve them one by one. Remember, guilt is adept at feeling "natural," so it can be hard to identify. Check in with your body to locate less obvious guilt feelings. Perhaps you experience a contracted feeling in your stomach when you must displease or disappoint someone. Unfortunately, no one can talk you out of the guilt you deeply believe you deserve. Your work is to decide, time and time again, that when you feel guilty, you will observe the feeling with the goal of determining whether it is appropriate or is stemming from your old way of thinking and seeing. For each guilt response you experience, ask yourself, "What am I feeling guilty about?" Then follow up with a reality check by asking, "Have I done something wrong?"

Also scan your answers for your personal patterns with guilt feelings. Patterns reveal what the lesson is.

Oddly enough, for many people guilt feelings result from not attending to their own needs. When you ignore your needs too long, you trigger an internal rebellion. This may take the form of overindulging in food, alcohol, sleep or nonproductive time. You set yourself up by overindulging and guilt smacks you down. A humorist once said, "Alcohol is its own punishment." To avoid this guilt trip, pay more consistent attention to your own needs. That way, rebellious overindulgence will not get many chances to occur.

Misplaced guilt feelings often strike when you're having a good time, feeling safe and loved. Guilt swamps your boat by reminding you of all those people who aren't as fortunate as you are. Here, your child-self feels guilty because it believes you should be performing for and satisfying others. That's the rule you break when you're enjoying yourself. This guilt has no basis in reality. It's coming from a child's fear of not doing enough to be loved. In reality, how does your enjoyment hurt others? Is there really only a limited amount of fun to be had? If you take a share, must others go without? When you were small, did your exuberance upset the adults? I once saw a mom on the beach admonishing her running, joyous child to be quiet!

EXERCISE 11-2

Casting Light on Guilt Feelings

☺ Create a statement that you can use to do a reality check when you notice guilt creeping up on you. For example, "Oh it's Guilt calling collect again! I'll refuse the charges!" Write your own statement and post it where you're sure to see it and use it — on mirrors, in the kitchen, in the car, at the office.

Fine-tuning the Guilt Response

You can't sustain guilt. Set a timer and just try to feel guilty about something for five full minutes. You can't do it. Guilt slips away like mercury on linoleum and returns when you drop your guard. It sneaks up and mugs you. Most adult guilt is unearned. You usually feel guilty when you are actually feeling responsible for the imagined response of others. Most people who are true wrongdoers don't experience guilt.

If you feel guilty even when no one has accused you of anything, remind yourself that you're paying a debt that you don't owe.

If someone does complain about your behavior, you have an opportunity to stay present and have a dialogue. If they complain about you to a third party, they're gossiping and that is no business of yours. Choose to remove guilt from your life and get your feet moving again. Remember, personal growth is spiritual growth!

Ferreting Out Fear

Now it's time to put fear in the spotlight, where it's most visible and vulnerable. You see, fear does its best work in the dark, behind the scenes, in your imagination. Fear is really sneaky. It robs you of your peace of mind while telling you it's for your own good! It can't stand the light. Let's take a look.

Fear is about control. How do others see me? Will I be enough? Will I get enough? What will happen if...? What did she mean by that? Where is it? Am I okay? Do you like me? Am I crazy? Will I ever have the answers? Am I doing this right? Fear questions go on and on, but you get the idea. The interesting thing about fear is that it doesn't wait for the answers. If you actually heard the question and reasoned it through realistically, you could return to inner peace. Then fear would be out of a job! So the questions keep coming. Fear keeps up its monotonous drone, relentlessly drumming just below your awareness, but definitely distracting you and draining your energy.

When you were small, the world was unfamiliar. You had many questions. Most of what happened around you was new to you and you had to fit it into a logical framework designed by your mind and your family's reasoning. You asked about everything. Sometimes your questions were received as annoyances. Sometimes no one answered them at all. You perceived that no one seemed frightened but you. You may have decided to keep your questions to yourself in order to measure up to what you saw as the "standard." So your fears, your questions about the world, were driven inward. You tried to figure things out on your own. Or you asked a sibling or a playmate for answers and got garbled information, or teasing, or both. The teasing shamed you, drove your questions deeper inward, and left you feeling even less safe in the world.

When children feel unsafe, they try to control their environment. They learn to manipulate others to behave in a predictable manner and they create safety rituals for themselves using thumbs, teddy bears or blankets.

Many of the unanswered fears remain unresolved. This predicament only creates more need to control to create safety. For the first two decades of life, when almost everything is new, life's learning curve is steep. The need to control such constant newness can be very powerful.

Reducing Fear

⊛ *You reduce or eliminate fear by revealing it, experiencing it and releasing it.* Once you have decided that fear is a constant but unnecessary part of your life, you have invited in lessons that will help you explore it. At first, fear will seem bigger than it really is. In reality, you have only "increased the volume" on what was already there. The monotonous low-level drone of "beware," "be careful," sounds like the truth because until now, you haven't been hearing it clearly enough to refute it. Once you can hear it, you can deal with it. It's like the monsters in your bedroom closet — huge in the dark and not there when you turn the light on.

EXERCISE 11-3

Transforming Fear

As you turn up the volume on your fear thoughts, record them in your journal for a week. Take no other action. Just record the scope of the Fear Mind. After a week, look for patterns. Where do you find fear most prevalent?

◊   Relationships

◊   Work

◊   Self-acceptance

◊   Physical safety

◊   Other

◊   Everything

Choose one area and begin consciously noticing fear thoughts. What are they saying to you? Are they true? Is there actual danger here? If danger is actually present, make sure to take care of your safety. But most likely, you'll find no impending harm. Here, fear is arises from the thought of possible harm based on the memory of past harm or the perception of harm. ☻ If there is no present danger, breathe gently into your body sensation (rapid heartbeat, clenched stomach, etc.) and feel the energy transform. Repeat this exercise as often as you experience fear to create a history of success for yourself. Experience the power you have over your own process.

EXERCISE 11-4

Give It To God

Everyone pursuing spiritual growth can practice this exercise regularly. When you encounter any automatic feeling response that's stopping your progress, ☺ give it to God or into the Light. Don't take it back! Give it freely, over and over, if need be. Feel God's willingness to lighten your load. There's no need to feel guilt about burdening God — God is not a human being who will be overwhelmed by your problems. God is universal life energy; limitless in size, strength and capacity for love.

Here's an example of how giving God your negative emotions can ease your journey. Suppose you are experiencing a recurring inability to communicate in your relationship. The two of you seem to speak a different language. In this case, all you truly know is your own internal process. "God, I give you my frustration. I give you my resentment. I give you my anger. I give you my inability to communicate with this person. I give you my fear of what this might mean. I give you my desire to blame my partner. I give you my pride that keeps me from exploring more deeply." As each feeling comes up, one by one, wave after wave, name what's appearing and give it to God. That's all. Use this release as often as needed. Don't keep count.

Letting unconscious fear run your life keeps you locked "safely" in your zone of familiarity. Fearful feelings don't want you to try anything new. In order to release the old ways of understanding and behaving, and to grow into new roles, lessons and knowledge, you must leave the zone of familiarity and enter uncharted land. Fear will do everything in its considerable power to stop your progress.

The zone of familiarity is like the shoes you wore in first grade when you learned all the rules. They are far too small for you now. Fear warns that these are the only shoes you'll ever get, that you'd better keep your big feet crammed into them.

Ask God to move in your life to help you leave those shoes behind. Move forward in faith that new shoes lie ahead — many pairs — in larger and larger sizes. Without shoes too small to move forward in, you will be lighter and rise above the feelings. Picture yourself rising up, taking your foot off your own oxygen hose, leaving the responses you've outgrown far below. Feel the freedom. The patient not only lives, she thrives!

Chapter 11
Tools For Guilt And Fear

❀   When you feel guilty, ask yourself whether you are actually harming someone. Then ask yourself if you are taking responsibility for their potential reactions.

❀   Decide, time and time again, that when you feel guilty, you will observe the feeling with the goal of determining whether it is appropriate or stems from your old way of thinking and seeing.

❀   Create a statement you can use to do a reality check when guilt creeps up on you.

❀   Reduce or eliminate fear by revealing it, experiencing it and releasing it.

❀   If there is no present danger, breathe gently into your bodily sensation of fear and feel the energy transform.

❀   Give your fear to God.

12

Forgiveness

To forgive is to free yourself from the burden of carrying everyone you have ever perceived as harming you in some way.

Let's explore how forgiveness truly is a gift and how you can give it to yourself. Imagine that someone has hurt you and you keep suffering repercussions of the pain he's inflicted. You may feel that you can never forgive him for wounding you so deeply. Perhaps you fantasize about "getting even" or making your victimizer suffer as much as you have. Or perhaps you feel your life is forever changed and you will never trust that kind of person or situation again. Once you've suffered enough of these wounds, you may decide to trust no one.

A broader perspective of hurt and forgiveness can help ease your way along the spiritual path. Holding onto the hurt is like holding your breath. When you're holding your breath, you can't do much of anything else. Even when you break down and take tiny little survival breaths, you hardly get enough oxygen to walk or talk. In the same way, when you hold onto your hurts, you can't move forward spiritually because you're focusing all your energy on keeping your wound intact. Part of you becomes an historian, curator of your personal museum of wounds. You actually hold yourself captive because your full energy isn't free to move forward. You do this to yourself quite unconsciously; and because it feels perfectly natural, you wouldn't be likely to question the behavior.

Make no mistake, forgiving in no way condones hurtful behavior. It doesn't mean you should go back and keep trying to get an apology or continue relationships with people who hurt you deeply. Letting go of incidents, deeds, or people in no way minimizes the depth of your injuries. The consequences of your victimizers' behavior and the contents of their hearts, remain between them and God. Keeping wounds alive in your own memory impedes your progress long after the painful incidents themselves are over. To move forward on a spiritual path, you must see how you alone are holding yourself captive to the memories of wounds. Your victimizers are out there, free, living their lives. You're not stopping them from hurting others by holding on to your pain. That said, let's take a look at some common responses to being victimized. Someone hurts you and...

Option 1

You "hold your breath" as you wish the person had never hurt you in the first place.

If only he hadn't hurt you, you wouldn't feel like a miserable failure all the time. An unevolved (young) part of the self is demanding that the past somehow be changed. Here you are holding your breath until the past is changed. How likely is it that you'll ever breathe again? No forgiveness is possible when you hold this perspective. Impossible conditions must be met first.

Option 2

You "hold your breath" as you wait for the offender to apologize and make appropriate amends.

You are holding on until your hurt is satisfied. Will it ever be satisfied? When someone says he's sorry, don't you find yourself waiting for more? What might "more" be? Without realizing it, many people use the following formula for forgiveness. They measure the amount of apology they receive against the degree of perceived injury plus the quality of expected attention, sympathy and acceptance they can gain from recounting the incident over the years.

Is it worth giving up your stories, your solicitation of sympathy, or your identity as a victim to let go of this wound and breathe again? When can forgiveness begin?

Option 3

You "hold your breath" until your victimizer suffers a fate as painful as yours.

There is no forgiveness here. It is a child's demand that life be fair. An eye for an eye. Would you want to deliver the revenge yourself? The truth is that whoever victimized you can never feel the hurt exactly the same way you do because he is not you. If you had learned from your wound, you would be unable to hurt another person in the same way you were hurt precisely because you know how horrible it feels to experience such intense shame, loss or fear. But the wound can teach you compassion for self and others.

Has your wound taught you anything? Do you forgive big incidents, but not small insults? Do you fight fiercely, but then feel devastated by cruelties done to you? Do you fantasize about your victimizer being sleepless, writhing in pain, or facing a firing squad? Are you holding your breath?

If you feel like a victim and believe you have a right to demand restitution, you don't have to forgive. Somebody's got to make it up to you. Somebody's got to make it better for you. With this belief, you are clearly giving away your power.

Option 4

You "hold your breath" until you understand why the offense happened to you.

The need to know why pain happens is one of the hardest things for people to let go of. Option 4 appears to contain forgiveness, (I'll forgive when I understand) but it really doesn't. Needing to understand another's motives or behavior (or even what happened to you in the past) is another of the mind's traps, and it's a trap that keeps you firmly in place, holding your breath. Chances are, you will never know the "why" of many life occurrences. Even if you were given reasons, they would be someone else's reasons, and would not make sense to you. As you try to decipher a rationale for your pain, you are still holding your breath, you are still at the mercy of your offender or some other outside force that you think holds the answers.

Option 5

All of the Above

You may feel that options 1-4 all fit, and fit well, so why would you want to give them up? When you do not forgive, you are surrendering your power until your victimizer returns it. You are holding your breath until she allows you to breathe again.

Clinging to your identity as a victim excuses you from succeeding, performing, or even showing up. It's hard to relate to the world in a positive way while you're holding your breath. You have no stamina. Your strength and endurance are limited. But you always have the excuse that you're holding your breath because you were hurt. Because you were hurt, you can't succeed (or grow, be happy, have a relationship, take care of yourself...).

There Is Hope!

Ultimately, who is hurt most by your breath-holding? Are the people who injured you losing sleep, gaining weight or feeling alone? Have their lives stopped progressing because of their hurtful actions? Probably not. What about your life? Has breath-holding become a familiar comfortable excuse not to achieve your full potential? Do you let your wounded places dictate how you spend your days on earth? If so, there is hope! When you acknowledge that what you have not forgiven is holding you back, perhaps even stopping you, you have taken your first step forward. You've recognized the barrier.

If you are not ready to take this step yet, let that be okay. (Remember, no judgment.) Go back and reread the chapter to this point. When you do, you'll be putting your intention out into the universe, letting God know that you want to be made ready and willing to let go. Read the next section, wait a few weeks and then read the chapter again.

When Wounds Feel Too Significant To Release

As you explore yourself, you may find that you're not ready to release some of your wounds. Please let that be okay. ☺ *There are no "have-to's."* There is no way to push it or force it to happen. You can release your wounds only when you're ready. God will know when you're ready and it will start to happen. You are in a process and you're not in control. Don't worry about it. It will come when it's time, and in the sequence of events you require for your soul's growth. Can you allow that much of a trusting attitude?

In many cases, wounds can feel so big and painful that in order to let go of them completely, people need to deal with each one in a safe place. Therapists and spiritual teachers can be very helpful in facilitating this effort. Be sure the chosen mentor can walk with you through this. To be of help, your guide should be able to forgive himself and to help you make a safe container for your process.

The need to hide what they imagine to be their deepest, darkest, most defective parts often keeps people from releasing and moving forward. They will be allowed to hide as long as they feel the need. Practicing woundedness makes it yours. But once you explore those "defective" parts one by one, you discover that you're all right (you're human) after all and you can move forward.

Now, if you have been feeling so suffocated that what you have been reading here feels like a gateway to freedom rather than a lecture on your inadequacies, read on. The best is yet to come.

EXERCISE 12-1

One Step Forward...

A woman once described feeling like she had bungee cords attached to her shoulders. She'd take one step forward, then spring way back into old feelings Let's look at some of the bungee cords holding you back. List in your journal the events or people you haven't forgiven and released. Refer-ring to our list of breath-holding options, record the numbers of the reasons you continue to hold in each case. Consider major and minor events. List everyone and everything you can think of. This is the first step in letting go. It's like raking all the leaves into one big pile. No judgments!

As you look over your list, notice if any patterns emerge. If your reasons for holding on tend toward one option, you have learned valuable information about yourself. ☺ *Look at this information not as a shortcoming to be corrected, but as an early warning signal to help guide your way.* When your thinking slips back onto that track, you'll be able to recognize it more quickly and stop yourself from staying with it very long. Make your list as thorough as you can. The goal here is to release, lighten up and be free. Shaming yourself about the length of your list defeats your goal.

Redefining Yourself

People often hold onto incidents because they seemed important when they happened. They never stop to reassess the value of past events. It's like running a museum that contains dozens of exhibits. No one has ever stopped and asked, "Do we still need this exhibit?" They keep it simply because it's there. They don't question it. If it's in a museum, it requires upkeep and security. Energy and money go into keeping the exhibit viable, even though no one may ever look at it.

Your museum of hurts and wounds comes to define you, to represent (in your mind) who you are. Your self-definition is the energy you take forward into the world. It's what you expect to find when you step out into your life. In the spiritual realm, all is energy. Thoughts are things, so whatever you think is what you manifest or have happen to you in your world. When you continue to define yourself by your "pain exhibits," you manifest pain. When pain appears, you say to yourself, "See I was right, I am a loser, I am a victim. I always attract this kind of person. I always have trouble with my jobs. I'm always poor...."

If you find these kinds of themes recurring in your life, are you willing to look at how you see yourself in the world? Are you letting your history define you? Are you willing to look at the possibility of opening your hands and letting go of those wounds, letting go of waiting for someone to make it better so that you can forgive? When you forgive, you free yourself, not the offender.

Spiritual beings are designed to change.

Once you stop defining yourself by your wounds, you are free to accept yourself as a spiritual being. On the spiritual path, you recreate yourself constantly. That's what spiritual growth is. Releasing, recreating, redefining, refining. Change is all there is because you're letting God define you. God doesn't see your woundedness. God sees only the spark of divinity in you, and waits patiently for you to see it, too.

When you accept that the process of spiritual growth is a lifelong process of redefining yourself, it becomes easier to stay on the path because you realize that this is how it's supposed to be. As a young child, you wear a certain size clothing and as you grow, the size changes. That's absolutely natural. You aren't expected to remain the same size forever. Growth and change are normal. Everyone is in the process of becoming, without knowing where it ends and if there are any limits. Limits are created only by the fear in our minds. Forgiving and letting go of past woundedness can release you into that becoming without demanding to know the outcome in advance.

Guideposts On The Road To Forgiveness

Saying you forgive and truly cleansing yourself of the wounds are two very different things. You may think you have released and moved on when remnants of those wounds are still interfering with your life. In some cases, you may want to forgive, but feel unable to do so. In other cases, you may believe you have released the wound but continue to feel stabs of resentment about it when life events trigger that psychic scar within.

To let go completely, use the Releasing Process described next. Don't be discouraged if you can't let go the first time through the checklist. No one I know can release completely in a single read-through. But as life events trigger memories of your wounds, you can use the Releasing Process again and again to help you keep moving. You'll be able to see how much more is left to clean out. Your goal is to free yourself, layer by layer, memory by memory.

The Releasing Process

1)   Notice When You Are Holding Resentment And Anger

Notice how your body responds when you get triggered by the name, smell, sound or other memory of a wound. You may notice a clench in your stomach. Your jaw or shoulders may stiffen. The body is often the best early warning system if you're willing to notice it.

On an emotional level, you'll find yourself getting angry, frightened or resentful. You may catch yourself muttering, "It's not fair, I hate her." All these kinds of responses are clues that you're holding on to this person or situation. I often think I'm finished with something and then somebody will innocently ask, "Do you ever hear from so and so?" Then, boom! The anger in my voice tells me I'm not through with that one yet!

Gauge your level of forgiveness by the degree of your emotional response to painful events. ☯ *Look at how intellectual understanding of the lesson and the teacher reduces your emotional response.* When you have worked through (not avoided) any held emotions, you begin to feel emotions in proportion to the current events triggering them.

2)   Understand And Accept That It Comes To You As Learning For Your Soul's Development

Painful experiences offer tools for refining our souls. One client learned to see that her mother, who was very narcissistic and cold, really taught her how to be strong. Once she let go of resenting her childhood, wishing she had a soft, cuddly mommy, and looking for a mommy in everyone, she came to realize that she had a lot of strength, resiliency and independence she wouldn't have had without that "unsatisfying" upbringing. After years of pain, she discovered her strength. She saw that if she could let go of that resentment, she could access her strength. She could continue to hold onto the wound or begin to nurture herself with that strength. She could change her focus. Another client described her fear of becoming a single mother and bearing sole responsibility for home and family. That fear kept her in her marriage. She was freed when she realized that she had been responsible for children, job and home for many years without her husband's support. After the divorce, her responsibilities continued, but her skills were already in place.

When you view the world as populated by teachers rather than by enemies, you can see how people's choices of behavior have strengthened you in the long run. No one said you asked to be abused, or that you have to respect your abusers, but you can choose to embrace the inner strength, independent spirit, compassion and wisdom you developed from experiencing those lessons. Will you stop relying on your woundedness as a reason for not moving forward? Will you accept your life and live it? Your life is now, not later, not after things are all resolved to your satisfaction. Since events in your past will never be resolved to your satisfaction, this concept frees you to live your life now, in the present moment.

3) *Pull Your Energy Away From The Event*

Each of the memories you hold requires energy to keep it alive. On the physical plane, it's a bit like collecting rocks every time you go on vacation. Each time you go, you collect half a dozen rocks. You feel attached to these rocks, but every time you move, you have to pack them up, haul them, unpack them, rearrange them and dust them. At some point, you have to decide how important it is to keep these rocks. Are they all special? Are they really necessary? How do they serve you?

When you release your energy from the original wounding event, you can consciously bring your attention to the current situation and notice:

    ◊ The original offender is not here

    ◊ There is no danger now

    ◊ I can handle this

Reassure yourself that you're fine now. Say the affirmation, "I claim my energy." Practice comforting yourself with the kind of comfort you so readily offer to others. Do this each and every time you find yourself having a negative emotional response to a person, event or memory. Take your energy back!

4) Acknowledge The Teacher Who Brings The Lesson

Some people are very quick to recognize an event as a life lesson, but they do nothing beyond that point. To go further, acknowledge the person who brought you this lesson as your teacher. This is an advanced step. It's important to realize that recognizing and acknowledging are not steps you can complete in one sitting. It's a process. If you remain willing, you'll be presented with opportunities to take each step. When you're ready, you'll be able to view everyone in your world, including your "enemies," as teachers.

Everyone you have ever met is a soul-level teacher who comes to you with lessons. You learn some lessons and you teach some lessons yourself. Some teachers stay a long time, teaching a specific lesson. Others come for brief encounters. I remember feeling very sorry for myself one day. I went to a fast food restaurant for comfort food. The young woman at the cash register smiled at me and I immediately felt blessed. Her smile was angelic and it filled my spirit. The food (yes, I ate it) tasted flat, but her smile lit up my life for the rest of the day. Even as I remember it now, I feel warmed. You will take what you wish from each encounter. Reflect on your life and extract the lessons. Remember to collect your rewards.

Everyone attracts people to help them work on aspects of themselves which need developing or refining. You draw to you the people you need. You may notice that the same kind of people repeatedly come into your life. Acting as your teachers, these people have free will, so they can teach in any way they want. Their kindness or cruelty is their expression of who they are. It's not about you. It's your interpretation of what's going on that determines how you receive the lesson.

My constant lesson, for example, has been learning to speak up to people whose voice and presence are demanding or attacking. I call these people "steamrollers" and I have always interpreted their every word as a command. I froze and forgot my own needs in a fear-driven desire to avoid making them angry. I placated, agreed and fawned, seething with inner resentment all the while. It never occurred to me to make my needs known to them. My interpretation of their behavior as angry and dangerous kept me a victim until I understood what their strong energy was offering to teach me about myself, and where I needed to grow.

If the lesson feels like one more victimization or one more episode of being misunderstood, then you're going to continue drawing those kinds of teachers, each of whom will offer the lesson in his own way. The universe is generous with the number of teachers it provides.

Once you've learned a particular lesson and defined the aspect of yourself that needs refining, your job is to work on cleansing your emotional response to the event. When your teachers provide lessons cruelly, you're left with the resentment, anger, pain and suffering that came with your interpretation of their actions. Healing and removing those feelings are a large part of the forgiveness process. Healing your interpretations will then be easier and future emotional responses will be less intense.

5) Collect Your Rewards

Once people get moving on the spiritual path, they often get so busy going from lesson to lesson that they don't stop to collect their rewards. If you skipped your graduation ceremony you wouldn't know you'd earned certificates for attendance, citizenship and penmanship. Then when you moved on to the next grade, you wouldn't be aware of your stellar skills, perhaps believing them to be at an unremarkable level. However, if you take time to notice how you're growing and changing, to rest and refresh yourself, you are better prepared for the next level of lessons.

If you feel unworthy, you're not going to remember to collect your rewards. Feelings of low self-esteem are often a result of painful life experiences or negative perceptions. *First, ask Spirit for a healing for your self-esteem!* Acknowledge, absorb, embrace and affirm your rewards. Only then will they become real for you. If you skip this step, you can have friends and family tell you how wonderful and creative you are, and it just slides off as if you were greased.

Collect your rewards. Acknowledge the gifts inherent in the learning. What have you come through with? Maybe a stronger sense of yourself. More independence. The ability to speak out in the face of anger? What have you gained from this series of lessons? Celebrate the strengths and use them.

EXERCISE 12-2

Taking a Look Inside

You are "becoming," which means you are learning, changing, realizing, awakening and growing. You are opening gifts of new understanding and ability within yourself. Take time to explore these gifts. This is an ongoing process and, though it takes time and effort, it shows you how far you've come.

Use your journal to write about changes you notice inside yourself resulting from life experiences. These are your rewards. Have you gained compassion, patience, honesty, serenity, strength of character, independence or the ability to forgive?

Consider redoing this exercise annually, perhaps on your birthday. As you open the gifts created by your learning and growth, you will experience support and renewal for the year ahead. Sharing your awareness with a spiritual group or counselor is a valuable way to reinforce who you are becoming.

6) *Release All Attachments To Remembering, Being Right, Being Justified Or Holding Someone Accountable*

Release your attachments. When you've been connected energetically to another person for a long time, they are probably also connected to you. When you've acknowledged that someone is your teacher and you want to let them go, you can detach from them using a meditation to surround them in golden light and say, "I release you." Saying this helps them let go of you, too. Remember, attachments bind more than one person. The attachment may take more than one meditation to sever. No judgments!

Quick pardons operate only in the head. They don't free your energy from attachment to the past. If someone offends you, let "that's okay" become a reality by following the Six-Step Releasing Process. Once you get a taste of the lightness of being that comes with releasing painful events, you'll have less tolerance for attaching any new threads that might hold you back. You may continue to perceive certain events as injuries, but with a new understanding, you'll have no need to hold on to that perception. You'll be truly free, with all your energy back in yourself where it belongs.

Taking The Broader Perspective

Using this view of forgiveness, can you accept that you have no control over what happens to you at the hands of others? When you accept that lack of control, your focus rightly returns to yourself. You can control only your interpretations of what happens. You can choose to see a bigger picture, filled with choices, free of blame. In this picture, you are in the driver's seat of your life, truly in control, in a way you had never imagined before. In this way, forgiveness is a gift you give yourself.

Chapter 12
Tools For Forgiveness

☙ There are no "have-to's," only choices.

☙ Look at information about yourself not as a list of shortcomings to be corrected, but as an early warning system to help guide your way.

☙ Intellectual understanding of the lesson and the teacher reduce your emotional response.

☙ Whenever you are feeling low, ask Spirit for a healing of your self-esteem.

13

Guidance

No one has "arrived" yet. We are all "becoming."
Accept yourself as a work in progress.

There are as many ways to be on a spiritual path as there are souls making the journey. There is no single "right way" to do the work. Although people do progress along their journeys alone, appropriate spiritual teachers can make the road a lot smoother. It's much like traveling for the first time from the Midwest to the ocean without a map. If you keep heading west, you'll eventually find the ocean, but if you have a map, you'll get there a lot sooner.

One of the challenges on the spiritual journey is choosing *which* map to follow. Some maps are more detailed than others. Some are topographical, which means you'll know the height of the hill you're going over, but you won't know the name of the highway you're on. Similarly, there are many kinds of teachers. Each spiritual teacher offers what he knows to be true, but his truth may not be your truth. His knowledge may guide you for a distance, but not the entire journey.

Find the people, books and classes that answer your questions. Be aware, however, that no single source can answer all your questions because that person's answers reflect their own path, not yours. Your work is to take what you hear from others and apply it to your own life, keeping what works for you and letting go of what doesn't. You're doing this work for you — it's your path, so individualize it. That's why no one person or group can dictate your process — unless you choose to surrender your will to them.

You will hear about dozens of different therapies and spiritual practices that people do, and be drawn to just one. It's a knowing, it's a recognition, an "ah-ha," not an "uh-oh." It's a pull toward that thing. Now this thing may not be the be-all and end-all of what you need. It may be just a small part of the overall picture. You may only need it temporarily and may eventually move on. You may find nothing you can use from a seminar, but you might come away with a new friend instead. Stay open to what's happening.

Finding Your Spiritual Map

People seek enlightenment in many ways and with many motivations. Our attraction to certain types of teachers and institutions is usually based on our upbringing. We tend to move toward what we knew as children — or to rebel against it. When people consider using organized religion as a spiritual map, they are often drawn either toward the churches their friends or parents attend, or to something totally opposite, such as Eastern religions, or Native American traditions.

It's helpful to look at why you've chosen as you have and to ask yourself if you're getting what you need spiritually from it. Or are you adapting your spiritual needs to what the religion wants from you? Some churches offer support and enlightenment. Many strongly support community giving and involvement. Other churches require that you attend services several times a week. Some demand absolute obedience to specific doctrine. Consider how fully acceptable *you* feel within your chosen traditions. Does the "real you" fit?

Charismatic Personalities

Spiritual leaders become famous because they speak and write well, they promote themselves well, and they speak truths that resonate in many people. Some people are so moved by what they hear that they want to pass the message along. "Have you read the latest book by so-and-so? Did you hear what she had to say about this? Did you hear her tape on that?"

There's nothing wrong with that kind of enthusiasm. But I caution you against taking anyone's entire dogma and swallowing it whole. Even mine. If you accept everything someone says as the ultimate truth, what will you do when parts of it don't fit your life? Where are you in this? Are you in the wrong? Instead, become a co-creator with Spirit. I encourage you to read famous authors and listen to what spiritual teachers have to say. Go to their lectures and workshops, take what you need and let go of the rest. You need to talk, to ask questions, and then to filter the answers through your inner wisdom to see what fits.

People who don't feel particularly solid in who they are tend to idealize others. They can be very drawn to religious figures. Some mystics set themselves up as demigods to be idealized. Be cautious if they claim that the Divine force emanates only through them, or if they demand complete dedication and obedience.

For some people being exposed to this idealization is like standing in a blinding spotlight. They can no longer see their own spiritual truth, and their dependence on someone else excuses them from thinking or reasoning for themselves. They respond to the nurturing parent setup and become "children."

Many of us grew up believing that we had none of the answers. Only adults, or doctors, or rabbis or priests had the answers. If you find yourself idealizing a religious figure, check in with yourself. Can you allow yourself to grow into the fullness of your adulthood and know that no one human has all the answers? To progress spiritually as an adult, you can allow others to assist in your journey, but you cannot let them become the journey itself. What's more, others can assist you only as far as they themselves have gone. And if the spiritual leader diminishes you in the process, he or she hasn't gone very far, despite appearances.

The Need For Acceptance

Why would someone give up their autonomy, individuality and awareness to another person or to a group? For many, the need to belong outweighs the desire for autonomy. When they're doing the rituals and wearing the costumes, when they're using the language of the spiritual practice they've adopted, they feel like they're special because they belong.

Some people do well living in ashrams and communes. They find that a structured path with limited choices is what they want. They feel safer when they live by someone else's rules and they're content with having someone else clear their spiritual path for them. If that's where you are, that's fine. There's nothing bad or wrong about it, it's just where you are. If you make that choice, however, stay aware enough that if at any point you outgrow that particular path, you can give yourself permission to leave. If the acceptance by a group is based on your complete obedience, that's very different than if this group accepts you because they're filled with acceptance.

Please notice if your feeling of belonging is one of belonging to this group, or of belonging to the Divine. The goal of joining a spiritual group is to assist you to raise your spirit to join with the Divine, not to enhance your social life or to ward off loneliness, though those may be current choices.

If you're in a group, check in with yourself and notice how much of you is welcome there. Can you be your full self in the presence of these people, or do you feel like you need to hide certain aspects of yourself? Do you have to hide your doubts about the group's practices in order to be accepted? If so, that's a clear indicator that your group is too narrow for you.

You can either find another group that's more open to individual experience, or ask yourself if it's time to walk your spiritual path on your own or with new teachers.

Your ultimate spiritual goal is to accept yourself for who and what you are just as God does.

Spiritual Tools

It's completely natural for people to want to use physical objects and activities as symbols to represent their spiritual concepts. Humans need to make the spiritual physical. It's done with pictures, crystals and statues or with activities like lighting candles, chanting, or wearing religious garb. Even with spiritual tools, remember that what fits today may someday be too small. Stay open and flexible.

Check in with yourself to see if the activities you're doing are working for you. Are they strengthening your sense of spiritual connectedness or are you doing them because someone else has dictated that you do them? Notice and make your own choices.

Drugs

People sometimes turn to mind-altering chemicals in the hope of achieving a spiritual experience. They believe that under the influence of certain drugs, they can be in direct contact with God. While this may appear to be so, it is a weak, fabricated connection.

On the spiritual path, there are no short cuts.

Even if you do open the doors to a spiritual experience using drugs, those doors will slam shut immediately as soon as the drug wears off, so nothing lasting is gained. And feeling locked out can be awfully lonely. There's also the real danger of opening too many doors in your psyche too fast and being unable to get back. Mental hospitals contain many folks who've lost their way. It happened more frequently in the 1960's, and it's still happening today.

If you've chosen to use drugs, ask yourself if they really have improved your spirituality. Has drug use really sustained you, or are doing it because other people have said it's a short cut to the Divine or as an escape route from yourself?

Suggestions For Selecting Your Spiritual Guidance

> As a general rule, when you're looking for spiritual guidance, look for teachers who are also students, not those who believe they are complete and in no need of guidance themselves. Look for humility. You might seek out people who seem to have qualities—like inner peace, compassion, or a sense of humor—that you admire and want for yourself.

Whether you're looking into a structured program — religious or spiritual — notice where you are within it. If you're following famous teachers, reading their books and listening to their audio tapes, remember not to embrace their answers as all the solutions to your spiritual needs. Take what you need from these potential teachings, and sit with it for a bit. Some of it will be very exciting. Some of it will be insightful. Ask yourself how much of it adds a measure to your life. Is it telling you who you are or teaching you how to become? There is a difference. You know who you are. A teacher can show you how to become what your soul wants to be.

Whoever you select as a guide, know that you were drawn there for lessons on some aspect of yourself. Maybe what you learn is that you don't like chanting or too much structure or solitary meditation. Let that new-found knowledge guide you to the next step in your spiritual education. Nothing is gained by feeling bad because you can't (or won't) meditate, for example. It's not a failing, it's where you are. Be there, without guilt or remorse, and discover for yourself what the next step is. Stay open to the natural flow of your lessons.

Instead of blindly obeying the catch phrases of the moment, like "go for the burn," I suggest that you continue discovering your way, your abilities and what you naturally move toward. ☺ *Notice and discard what is not productive or beneficial for you.*

Inner Guidance: How Do You Know Which Practice to Embrace?

Imagine yourself in a garden filled with every kind of flower on earth. Some are incredibly beautiful, but when you get close, they have thorns, or they don't smell good. You're allergic to others. One contains a large bee. And some, upon closer study, look beautiful to other people but not to you.

You don't have to gather every flower in the garden to make a bouquet. Pick the ones you like. They will suit you perfectly. As one blossom or another begins to wilt, discard it. You can replace it if you choose, or you can find something different. Be sure to change the water every few days because as the water becomes cloudy, it no longer sustains the flowers. Similarly, emotions like fear, resentment and guilt can cloud your thinking and prevent you from maintaining your spiritual connection.

You "choose your flowers" for your bouquet by taking what you learn from your guides and filtering it through the wisdom of your higher self. To become acquainted with your higher self, you need to quiet your mind. Inner guidance, meditation, prayer, stilling the mind, and listening to the Heart are all vehicles that can take you down the same road. The following section will help you find a method that fits you.

Meditation

In our busy culture of coming and going, doing and achieving, many people say they don't have time to sit quietly and still the mind. That's only because it hasn't yet been set as a personal priority. People usually decide to make quiet time a priority when everything else has failed, when they hunger deeply for spiritual connection and have not been able to find it *any other way*. That is when they come together in groups to meditate, or in churches to pray.

I will describe meditation in general terms and would suggest your finding a teacher or group if you wish to learn a specific form like Transcendental Meditation or Zazen. Learn about structured forms of meditations, but if the rules don't work for you, or if the content of the meditation doesn't work for you, don't force yourself into a mold. Build a history of success to replace the history of failure. Meditation is whatever you experience it to be. It is not a series of peak experiences. It isn't always relaxing. The first time you do it, you may have a strong, moving experience. You may never experience those kinds of blissful feelings again. They weren't the point anyway.

Meditation is the process of quieting the mind and listening to your inner guidance. The point is to get the mind so still that you can see what's there. If what's there is ants in your pants, then that's what's there. If what's there is the awareness that you can't put the thoughts out of your mind, or you hadn't realized your back hurts, or your feet ache, then you've received something from it, haven't you? The goal is to know yourself and what you're holding, not to impress anyone with your powers of concentration. The goal is to go within.

Going within is done through the breath. Your breath is the pathway to your higher self, your individual truth. You don't need to be "taught" to breathe. You already know that. What you may need to learn is to sit with your breathing. Your breath will empower you to attain mastery over your life, over the lessons you draw to you. Breathe quietly into the silence and go within for answers, for healing and for rest. You will see changes in your outer life. The changes may be slow and subtle, but they will occur. Consciously sitting with your breathing lets you notice it.

By being conscious of your breathing, you automatically let go of the world around you, as well as all of its transient problems. If you don't believe problems are transient, take a moment to notice what you were worried about last month, or even last week. Haven't those concerns for the most part faded and been replaced by new worries? Be aware that you can make your life an endless string of worry beads. If you want to attain conscious living and inner peace, you can choose to drop the string of beads for awhile each day as you go within. Your concerns will sit quietly at your feet, like an old dog waiting for its master's return. But with worries, who is the master? Meditation can help you see which situations you have any influence over. I used to have a sign to remind myself that "I have lived many years. I have had many troubles, most of which never happened."

It does take some discipline to carve out five, 10 or 15 minutes for yourself every single day. But to meditate, you need to commit to sitting quietly, no matter what. When you begin sitting in silence, you need to find a quiet place where you won't be disturbed. Close doors so pets can't come and join you. They're very drawn to peacefulness. Turn off the ringer on the phone and tell family members that you need quiet for meditating.

Find the same spot in your home to sit each time you meditate. When you use the same pillow or chair, your meditative energy begins to accumulate in that place so that when you sit there, your mind will automatically start to settle down. If you want to turn that area into your special place with a candle or sacred objects that add to your quiet time, you can do that, but it's not required. The nice thing about meditating is that it doesn't cost anything. The only real requirement is your presence. It's too free for some people, but there it is.

How often should you meditate? It's up to you. Some groups suggest about 20 minutes twice a day, while other people go on week-long retreats where they do nothing but sit in silence and meditate. Still others do walking or moving meditation, which includes repetitive motion that induces a gentle trance state. Do whatever works for you. There are lots of books out on types of meditation. The purpose is to go inside yourself without worrying about how you're performing or what the rules are.

Prayer is talking to God and meditation is listening.

I like that saying because when we pray, we're very busy talking. "God, I want this. God, please help that person..." When we're talking, we're not listening. We're not hearing the still, small voice within that might be saying, "Her cancer is terminal. It's time for her to go." And knowing that could be quite comforting. Human will resists change, discomfort and emotions. Divine will accepts what is and helps us to accept that, too.

Support Your Process

You'll need to support your rational mind with information to reassure and comfort yourself while doing your daily spiritual work and waiting for what doesn't seem to be showing up. Because the spiritual process and Divine Spirit cannot be seen, heard, held, tasted or touched, the reasoning mind has a hard time holding on to it. The more you educate your reasoning mind, the less fear will block it.

Different people need differing amounts of information to put them at ease. Remember, you are growing now. You are changing, naturally and subtly. Information (books, tapes, etc.) that you select today may go untouched for awhile. You need to grow into readiness. Suddenly, that book will seem like something you want to explore. It doesn't matter if this information (or author) has been popular for eight weeks or 800 years. When it's right for you, your attention will be drawn to it. In the following exercise, you'll explore the use of meditation as one of the keys to learning about yourself.

EXERCISE 13-1

Finding What's Right for You

Ask yourself why you are trying to meditate. List every reason that comes to mind. Your list could look something like this:

1) My teacher (or group) requires it.

2) Everybody is doing it except me.

3) It looks so "spiritual."

4) Praying is talking to God and meditation is listening.

5) For stress management.

6) I'm strongly drawn to carving out spiritual time for myself.

7) Stilling my mind.

Your responses will guide you to the next step that is right for you. Learn to distinguish what you "should" do from what feels right.

Choosing either "should" or "feels right" brings lessons. Ultimately, there really are no mistakes. However, being in touch with our inner guidance cuts down on a lot of detours. As you cruise down your spiritual highway, all exit ramps look much the same and it's easy to get off on a side road. You'll see a lot of different scenery that way, but your trip will take longer. As you come to know yourself better, *through your choices and your feeling responses*, you'll be better able to stay on track.

EXERCISE 13-2

List your current spiritual practices

List all your spiritual practices (like the affirmations you use while brushing your teeth, the daily meditation book you consult, or the talisman you wear).

Now, go back over your list and mark each practice with an "S" for something you feel you should do, or an "R" for something that feels right to you. Do you notice any patterns here? Are your rituals designed to ward off fear? Do they show your desire for a lot of structure? Or do you find that you have very few spiritual practices?

As we progress along a spiritual path, we usually start with something that's structured and external, like tangible spiritual practices. Later, we move toward an internal focus on what those teachers and practices teach us about ourselves. We tend to live from the outside in until we realize that everything has the potential to be a sign pointing inward. The process is somewhat like closely examining a rose. The first thing we notice is the color, then the external petals. How open is it? Not until it has opened completely can we get to the heart of it and really enjoy the fullness of its essence.

Knowing who you are
Is better
Than living a life
In lonely desperation
Waiting for someone
Who never appears
To save you
From yourself.

Staying on Your Path

Here's an example of what I mean by living from the outside in, of hearing the concerns of others over your own. Suppose you are in a relationship with a partner or co-worker who brings you lessons about not rescuing others. This person always seems to be faltering or hurting and you quickly offer to bear their load by offering solutions, intervening for them or worrying about their problems. As you come to see these "rescue efforts" are detours from your path, you can remind yourself not to take them. Rescuing someone may feel like the right thing to do in the moment, but in reality, it sends them the message that they are too weak or helpless to do the task themselves. What is meant as love is really interference in someone else's learning. The other person continues to feel weak and dependent, without learning how to handle things their own way and comes to depend on the rescuer more and more. As a rescuer, at first you feel good and competent, but after awhile you're bound to feel resentful and trapped. You may notice how the "victim" you're trying to rescue ignores your help or always needs your time and attention. Now who feels like a victim?

I suggest you skip that detour next time. Don't go there, don't feel all that crummy guilt. Just realize that this is where your work is, releasing the guilt. Look instead at your ever-rising standards for your own behavior and, see how you've filled your time so much with the needs of others that your own needs have become orphans. Look at your over-full calendar. Is there any time scheduled for you? How will you hear your inner wisdom if you never have time to listen? Sometimes the only thing that stops an overdoing person is illness. Even then some people refuse to rest, bringing their germs to work or school with them. Or, even if they do stay home, once they feel better, they jump back in with both feet before their body has fully recovered.

Our culture teaches people to ignore their own needs. Motivational phrases for athletes tell us to "Go for the burn," "Work through the pain," and "Beat your personal best." Rather than perpetuating your pain, I suggest you continue discovering your way, uncovering the practices and impulses that don't support your spiritual path and identifying those that do. Does all this focus on yourself make you a selfish person? About as selfish as a car that requires fuel and regular maintenance in order to provide reliable transportation. Commit to taking care of yourself as well as you care for your machines.

Somehow, the teachings of the great religions of the world have come to be interpreted as requiring giving with no thought of receiving. Yet unless you take the time to receive from God, what is it that you're giving? If you don't learn to receive from others, how do they learn to give? When religious or spiritual leaders talk about total giving with no thought of receiving, they're talking about an ideal. They're talking about something to work toward, a time when you are filled with spirit and no longer need much from the world. Not there yet!

As a student of spirituality, you are working toward the highest standards. Just don't expect to accomplish them all in one lifetime! Work on knowing yourself with compassion and refining the aspects of yourself that need attention. Seek guidance along the way.

Chapter 13
Tools For Guidance

❧   When you're looking for outside guidance, look for teachers who are also students.

❧   Notice and discard what is not productive for you or
not beneficial to your needs.

14

Refinement

Life is the place in which to make mistakes
so that refinement is possible.

There are assignments for souls at every level of development. Every one of us is a student, whether we're aware of it or not. No one is ever finished, no one is ever perfect. Yet the process is.

As you become more clearly aware of how you treat yourself—as you exercise compassion, willingness and patience with yourself and release anger, judgment and control — you will be ready to listen to the echoes of your heart. You will begin to fully appreciate the value of sitting in the silence. In the silence, if you allow yourself to notice, you will recognize where you are in the process of opening and releasing.

When you sit in silence, is there a restlessness, a thought that you could be wasting your time, or that you'll never "get it?" Do you occasionally enter a higher place that leaves you wanting to return for more? If you practice sitting daily, ignore such inconsistencies and don't judge your performance. Consider allowing yourself this daily respite to invite your higher self to speak to you. Let this time period adjust itself to what seems right for you. Release all need to be doing something concrete. Just let yourself be.

As you refine yourself spiritually, you are in the process of healing the very fibers of your being, one at a time. In a woven cloth, single fibers are not visible. However, a broken strand or two, several off-color threads or knotted fibers are quite noticeable. Seeing, understanding and repairing the fabric of your being is delicate, painstaking work that becomes easier as you learn how to do it.

At first, you will stay in touch with the inner silence only during your brief meditation sessions. Eventually, though, you will notice that the inner silence remains with you during your daily activities. You may find yourself feeling less anxious in a particular situation, less concerned about being out of control in another. This peaceful awareness grows over time if you keep at the practice of being in silence. Once you focus on your soul's work, the benefits permeate your entire life, first on the spiritual plane and then in your physical experiences. It isn't easy to discipline yourself this way. There are many distractions, often manifested as fearful thoughts. Assure yourself that there is no reason to delay. Start now. Look with compassion at how you have been holding yourself back from all the spiritual gifts that are rightfully yours.

Above all, have patience with yourself on this journey. If you aren't already a patient person, many lessons will be sent to teach you this valuable skill! The Divine Spirit awaits you, but does not judge. ✆ *Each time you are given an opportunity to learn a lesson, your free will enables you to make a new decision by realizing your old knee-jerk decision is not helpful.* Your higher self will help you with this process. You are never alone.

Human beings aren't the only energy that exists. In fact, we are really only a small part of the universal energy, but everything on earth exists in service to our spiritual growth. This is our school. That makes us seem tremendously important, doesn't it? Yes, it does. We are that important. Many of us don't understand just how powerful and important we humans really are. Understanding this is part of our overall spiritual lesson on the use and abuse of power. Consider the role of animals in our lives. They are on earth in selfless service to humans. (Stay with me on this.) They sacrifice their lives so that we can eat. They sacrifice their lives in inhumane traps so that we can learn about suffering and stop causing it. Their skin has been used to clothe us, but as we find other ways to make clothing, we're beginning to see the senselessness of killing animals for their skins. As we discover new ways to nourish ourselves, we realize it's unnecessary to eat their flesh. We're beginning to recognize that it's not best for the animals to put them in zoos — they do much better in their natural habitats. We are extremely upset when another culture poaches a species into extinction.

So, in their service to us, animals are teaching us come closer to love. Love isn't having power over someone or something else, it's learning to live together, sharing the planet. In this way, over the years people have used (and continue to use) animals as teachers for spiritual evolution.

As you change your perceptions, beliefs and behaviors, an unconscious way of living is no longer in control and an "aware self" emerges. Notice that this new self is guiding with love, rather than prodding with fear. The difference in approach may feel foreign to you. You will begin to experience longer moments of inner peace. You will become more attuned to your inner nature. You are quietly listening, not performing.

But then the mind switches on, shaming you for your lack of visible productivity. The mind will urge you to become unconscious again. Remaining conscious or returning to remote control is a choice at your fingertips every moment. You can change your mind at any time, without judging yourself. When you become aware of the inadvisability of a choice, simply choose again. The time you spend in regret or self-judgment is of no use. You may judge yourself for judging yourself for judging yourself... into oblivion. Or you can let go of self-judgment. You can hold the situation lightly, treat yourself lovingly, and move on.

The Fear Mind aches to make this process of letting go more complicated than it is. The mind wants you to believe there is some magic formula that others possess, but that you can have only after you have managed to please everyone else! This crippling belief controls you only as long as you remain unaware of it. Following it makes you an unconscious prisoner of self-judgment. Your mind becomes filled with constant chatter: lists of things to do, admonitions for self-improvement, warnings of the consequences of failure, and urgings to "hurry up."

When you live an unconscious life, even spiritual practice is turned against you. Fears of God's retribution, karmic consequences, and not being spiritual enough can haunt your days. Spiritual practice can become an unpleasant chore or a competition about who can meditate longest, levitate highest or perform the most spectacular miracles.

⊚ *Remember that spiritual practice is the process of enhancing inner peace and soul growth in a loving manner.*

You are doing it wrong only if...

◊ The voices in your mind are criticizing you with words of fear about your performance

◊ You are comparing your progress with the progress of others

◊ You are judging any part of it

Choose Again!

Once you become aware of the elements of spiritual practice, you can make more conscious choices. Lessons and guidance will be available to you either way. This is Divine Justice.

Each lesson you learn refines an aspect of your soul and moves you closer to God. As you become more refined, you become sensitive to ever slighter imbalances. In the early stages of spiritual growth, for example, you might be in a battering relationship and realize that you need to leave it. Once you've learned to say no to physically abusive relationships, you may notice that some of your other relationships are emotionally abusive. You may choose to end them. You may realize that some friends are insulting and critical. You could challenge their behavior, because you will no longer tolerate it.

As you become more aware of what's happening in your relationships, you develop an interpersonal radar that picks up increasingly subtle signals and alerts you to unhealthy behavior. You can learn a great deal about love from its absence. And you will become more and more aware of issues that are unfinished for you. They will keep calling your attention because your soul is urging you to do the work it takes to finish them. This is refinement.

Keeping your eyes open and taking responsibility for your life is all it takes to keep refining your development. You harm no one in doing this. It brings glory to God. The saying "Your life is God's gift to you — what you do with it is your gift to Him" couldn't be more true. Let your heart absorb this reality. Let your answers come from you, not from others. Be true to your higher self and all will be in Divine Order. Open your life like the gift it really is and live out your appreciation. Move forward in faith, one foot in front of the other.

Chapter 14

Tools For Refinement

⊛ Your free will enables you to make a new decision every time you realize an old decision is not helpful.

⊛ Spiritual practice is the process of enhancing your inner peace and soul growth in a loving manner.

15

Being of Service: Where Do I Start?

Do your own work first...
so that the teachings that come through you are authentic.

St. Augustine wrote, "Fill yourselves first and then only will you be able to give to others." Somehow this approach has gotten lost through the ages. Today, it's "Give 'til it hurts. Forget your petty little needs. " My personal favorite is, "I cried because I had no shoes 'til I saw a man who had no feet." In trying to teach compassion for others, this motto ignores compassion for yourself. In effect, it says everyone else is more important than you, that you can't ask for anything until everyone else has enough. But why is your lack of shoes any less deserving of attention than someone else's lack of feet? How is ignoring your cold, shoeless feet helping anyone else? Unless you acquire some shoes, you too, might lose your feet.

My meaning here is: Don't jump into being of service just because you perceive others to be in pain. To become ready for service, you need to understand this. Once your spirit has enough nourishment, you'll be able to give from the heart, rather than from a sense of guilt or obligation. Let's look at this idea in more detail.

I believe the widespread concepts of altruism and self-denial grew from a belief in limited supply, only so much food, only so much love, and so on. When supply is seen as limited, you have to share your portion with others to be considered a good person. But if supply feels limited to you, you may have carried forward the childhood perception that sharing means giving it all away. Many a child was taught to give her toy to another child who reached for it. One toy doesn't stretch to satisfy two children. It's all or nothing.

You may also be retaining the childhood belief that you have been "bad" and must now "go to your room." This is the learned concept of self-denial. If you were exiled from the family (or TV or your toys) as punishment, you learned to equate displeasing others with not deserving what you had just a moment before. Without realizing it, as an adult you may be punishing yourself with self-denial because you've failed to live up either to your culture's "rules" or the standards of behavior that were programmed into you during childhood. In this way, your giving to others can be driven by a core belief in your basic badness and a desire to appear good. Have you ever given more than you wanted, trying to please someone who may not have wanted what you were offering? When this happens, your gift feels like a failure and, the more you appear to fail, the more you give — and the more you resent the giving. Most of this is happening at an unconscious level. One example is people who won't give money to homeless people because they might use it to buy drugs or alcohol, or because they don't say thank you. A homeless person may want your money, but not your values. If you aren't giving with open hands, why are you giving? Does guilt push you to give in the first place?

Add to this the religious standard that tells you to give without thought of receiving. But unless you take time to receive from God, what is it you're giving? When religions talk about giving with no thought of receiving, they're describing an ideal, something to work toward. But they rarely tell you how to get there! You may well feel like the only one who is inadequate to the task. Thus, whatever you do or give, it's not enough. You need a wider understanding of giving and receiving. You need to heal first.

Filling Up, Then Flowing Outward

The spiritual healing process helps you learn to receive from God because God is the source. If you allow yourself to be nourished and fed, not only by Divine love but your own compassion and attention to yourself in the moment that your needs arise, you're drawn to your acts of service naturally, without desire for reward, because the giving becomes its own reward. But realize that this feeling, too, is an ideal. The first step is to feed yourself, be loving to yourself, and allow God to feed you, too. Like they say on the airlines, ☺ *Put on your oxygen mask first, then assist others."*

The message throughout this guidebook for the soul's journey to enlightenment is to attend first to yourself and then flow outward. This is a different concept of being of service. When you don't know who you truly are, you won't be able to be of service to others. Your giving will be driven by emotions like guilt instead of Divine direction. As you grow in self-knowledge and self-caring, you will recognize meaningful ways to be of service. So the first area to explore is your ability to fill up, to receive. Let's return to the "old saw" about shoes and feet. Based on your discomfort, you could simply notice that you had no shoes. Or, you could allow yourself to find, buy, trade, make or ask for shoes to relieve your discomfort. Once you get the shoes you need, you can come from a position of fullness and be much better able to give to others.

As one who has learned to ask and to receive, you are better qualified to teach those lessons to others. It's the same with emotional and spiritual fullness. Attend to each aspect of yourself. ☺ *When you're open to noticing and attending to your emotional and spiritual needs moment by moment, you learn to ask and begin to receive.* Gradually, you fill up. If you don't attend to your own needs and can't ask anyone to attend to you, you just may starve. God wants you to have all you need. There is enough for you. Ask for what you need, open your receptors and you will begin to fill up. How will you know when you are full enough and are ready for service? By living in the world and noticing your responses and reactions. Filling, like receiving, is a steady process, not a onetime event. Sometimes you will need more and other times less. How rapidly you accomplish self-caring depends, in great part, on your commitment to spiritual growth and how consistently you love yourself. Asking starts the flow. Being receptive to it keeps it coming.

Ask God for what you want.

Because you are given free will, God cannot give you anything until you ask. He can force nothing on you. If you hold the belief that you must do something all by yourself, you are cutting yourself off from the universal source and will find the going difficult. And it is your choice. The freedom of adulthood offers you many sources of self-enrichment. Here's an old bit of truth, "Don't put all your eggs in one basket." In other words, don't expect one person to become your world and fill all the wounded or empty places within you. As an adult, you can notice what you need from moment to moment. You can create solutions by asking, seeking and noticing what's available. If you're bored and restless, having your partner or child entertain you is only one option. Other choices might include taking a nature walk, doing a creative project or shopping for a shut-in. What other options are there for you? Use the next exercise as an opportunity to go inside and ask!

> ## EXERCISE 15-1
>
> ### Options to Fill My Needs
>
> *Write down what you do to fill your needs now, as well as actions you'd like to take to support yourself. Make sure to consider physical needs, emotional needs, mental needs and spiritual needs.*

Yes, you are responsible for noticing your needs. You are also responsible for filling them! Remember, you are drawing from God's unlimited supply. Keep asking until you feel filled. Each person will need differing amounts. Some days you will feel full and other days you will feel needy.

Taking from an unlimited supply does not deprive anyone.

Isn't that beautiful? There's no one to blame if you're feeling empty. Instead of falling into the victim trap, work on your ability to receive. Just notice the feeling of emptiness and get into action! Use one of the actions you listed above to get started. Open to receiving and let God work through you. When you have allowed God to fill you, you will feel ready for service. It will feel natural and effortless.

Cutting Yourself Off From The Source

There's another aspect of not having and not asking which comes from believing in limited supply. In Chapter 6, I used the metaphor of a wall socket covered by a child safety cap. Electricity is still available, but the cap prevents you from plugging in your lamp, so you eventually forget that the electricity is even there. In a similar manner, even though people may love you and offer you gratitude and compliments, when your receiving socket is blocked, demonstrations of love slide off and can't reach your heart. You won't allow yourself to have love, so you don't even perceive it! And when you aren't aware, you perpetuate your sense of limited supply. I'm reminded of a person so caught up in the loss of a love relationship that she couldn't see or take in the love and support offered by family and friends.

When you continually frustrate those who love you by deflecting their affection, they may eventually give up. It doesn't matter whether you have difficulty receiving because you feel unworthy or because you feel more comfortable being the one who is giving. Here's something to think about. When you give constantly, you deny others the opportunity to learn to give. There is arrogance and imbalance in being the only giver. The position strongly implies that what others offer is of little worth, that yours is the only valuable gift. Of course, this isn't your intention. But when you are this out of balance, you can't see how the other person feels. One-way giving comes from your need, and ignores the needs of others, like the Boy Scout "helping" the lady cross the busy street whether she wanted to or not. The bottom line is this: You can't be of service, in the true sense of the word, unless you are in balance. That is, unless you can also receive.

EXERCISE 15-2

Practice in Receiving

Use this exercise to explore what you already receive from others. If you have been open only to giving, you may want to use this exercise to consider what you could allow yourself to receive. For example, do you allow yourself to ask for and receive a hug from your partner when you're feeling sad? Do you open your heart and allow yourself to receive a genuine compliment from a friend? Will you allow someone to buy you a meal, to surprise you with a gift? List in your journal who gives to you and what you receive.

Remember, if everyone gave without receiving, who could you give to? How about allowing others a chance to learn to give — to you! That may be a service to that person. Everyone gains intrinsic benefits from giving. Don't deny this to others.

There is plenty of need on this planet and a wide variety of givers. All the world's tragedies aren't yours even if you do tend to clutch them to yourself. This is a valuable gift from your guidance, if you'll listen. Meditate on it.

Opening Yourself To The Source

☺ *Do what your heart is drawn to and leave the rest for other spiritual students to attend to.* If you allow yourself to remember that there is limitless electricity available behind your personal "safety cap," you can start taking a close look at the cap itself. You need to know what the block is made of. You don't necessarily need to know how it got there, but you need to know what it consists of. Is it made of guilt? Is it made of anger and resentment? Pain and suffering? What do you need to do to remove the cap and open yourself to the Source so that love can flow again? Don't expect to remove the safety cap in a single effort. It is a process. You may ask for clarity about what is blocking your love from flowing into you. ☺ *Hold the intention that you really do want to know the answers.* Once you ask and remain quietly aware, the answers will begin to present themselves. The block will probably come apart in pieces, because it's not really a single solid object. You have to keep at it, releasing piece by piece, until the entire block is removed.

Your Growth
Influences The Growth Of Every Other Soul

Believing God's bounty is limited causes people to hoard, hold on and contract. Holding on like this hurts the one doing the holding. Yet what began from fear of lack is now labeled "selfishness." How can you consider yourself selfish when God has designed the entire universe for the benefit of all souls? By knowing who you truly are and by helping yourself achieve your highest potential, you are actually benefiting humankind. When one soul grows, all souls grow because in God, all are one. When one soul falls, all souls suffer and must work harder to grow and heal. Here's an example of that concept. People who choose a criminal path have a powerful impact on the choices you make about your life-style. You may feel like you have to avoid certain neighborhoods entirely, or you may feel fearful about driving a new car or wearing expensive jewelry. You may feel unable to enjoy the material rewards you've worked hard for.

A change in your world view may draw you to a path of service. Your desire to get beyond the fear can lead you to helping others get beyond their fears. Evolved souls may be drawn to create programs to build better communities or help criminals realize that what they're doing is not acceptable. They may encourage those who have fallen to see that they can grow and change. The existence of criminals influences law-abiding citizens who in turn can effect not only the criminals, but the community at large. There are so many opportunities to give service, and so many souls who benefit by it.

All souls are connected. When you work on your own growth, your healing energy will pass on to those in need. As you become strong enough, you can also help on the physical plane. However, trying to be of service to people in agony before you heal yourself will lead to defeat. When you try to heal others before you're healed, your heart still carries old wounds and fears that make you want to rescue them from their pain. And rescuing isn't helpful.

Compassion and support in the form of soul-to-soul understanding are called for here. It's not helpful to block someone else's path of learning by being their rescuer. Others are exactly where they need to be to learn the lessons they need to learn this time around. From this perspective, "saving people from themselves" is the height of arrogance. Stay on your own path. You have a big enough job to do there.

Service is different from helping. When you help someone, you use your resources and may feel more powerful, like giving advice to a friend when your life is going smoothly. This is the business of the ego, which likes to feel in charge and wants results, much like that "helpful" Boy Scout. When the ego is involved, it wants gratitude and recognition for giving. It wants the other person to change! Service, on the other hand, evolves from who you are rather than what you have or can do. It comes from a place of humility and gratitude. Serving fills the servant. It offers what it has and lets go of outcome.

Let's not overlook that acknowledgment and gratitude for deeds and thoughtfulness are important. After all, humans are in a community of spirits and need each other. We need to say thank you. The goal is not letting go of the need to be thanked, it's finding your own way to be of service. Notice if your helping tends to come from a desire to be acknowledged or accepted. To gauge whether you can be of service to someone else, ask yourself if you can really offer something here, or do you need to accept reality and let God handle the situation?

Give Genuinely, From Your Heart's Desire

Look at your behavior in this light. Teaching others to care for and about themselves is far superior to doing it for them. You can teach by example and deed. You can project love and compassion and you can let go into Divine Order. Your inner guidance will lead you. But first, you need to spend time in the silence so you learn to distinguish your authentic inner voice from the all the other voices in your head (who are also advising you about what to do).

When your higher self offers guidance, your heart will respond. The work you choose may be easy, light and joyous. You will probably feel full and fulfilled. This means that it's better not to take on a task just because you know how to do it, especially if the work isn't something you like to do. Don't bring resentment with you into your service. There are many needs in the world. You can find the ones that you will enjoy serving. Other people will step in where they are needed. All who are open to receiving can be served. The key is openness to receiving!

With so many needs to choose from, you may find it difficult to set limits on your giving. Each voice, each charity, each nation and each disaster may call out to your heart, so it can be hard to decide where to direct your limited time and resources. Years ago, I received some guidance on this from a wise woman. She suggested limiting the donation of time to three causes per year. Your choice may vary from year to year, but the limit stays the same. I've added a limit for myself on monetary donations.

With much thought, I selected ten causes I felt good about supporting and that's where my charitable giving goes. In addition, I allow myself to stay flexible in case there's a pressing need in my own community.

Perhaps all this feels too vast (or expensive) for your resources. The idea of consciously selecting where you dedicate your time and money is to enable you to see that you are helping, you can't do it all alone, and guilt is an unnecessary burden. Remove guilt by acknowledging what you do. Let that be enough.

When you are living your truth, those around you will feel inspired to rise to a higher level. The recipients of your service, if you choose to be of service, will owe you nothing, because your offering will come from your heart, not your ego, and your heart already will be full from the doing. This is how everyone is served. It is easy to say and difficult to do. Much work must be done clearing out old beliefs about service and giving. Work gently with yourself.

God does not expect humans to be perfect. God insists on nothing. Only your ego demands that you be perfect. Your soul demands growth. Which demand will you choose to direct your life?

EXERCISE 15-3

The Power Of Offering A Prayer

Here's a way to be of service. While you are working on clearing yourself to gain greater balance, you can be helping others. Here's an activity for daily or occasional use.

Think of all the people and conditions you would like to have a positive effect on. Include your own name and your own issues. Write each one on a small slip of paper and fold twice. Place all the folded papers in a container.

As often as you choose, select one paper. Then spend a few minutes picturing this person or situation in Divine Order, which means imagining that God is in charge and that everything is happening exactly as it should, not as you will it. Send it Light and Love and ask God to bless it. Thank Divine Spirit for assisting in this matter and return the name to your container. Now let go. Worrying and thinking about results pulls back the positive thoughts you've been sending out. Trust God to know what's needed and to do it. As new people or situations arise in your awareness, add them to your container. If one item comes into your hand frequently, know that it needs more attention.

Chapter 15
Tools For Being of Service

❧   Put on your oxygen mask first, then assist others.

❧   When you notice and attend to your needs and wants, moment by moment, and learn to ask for what you want, you begin to feel fuller, and you gradually fill up.

❧   Do what draws you from the heart and leave the rest for other spiritual students to attend to.

❧   Once you ask for guidance and remain quietly aware, the answers will begin to present themselves.

16

Following Your Own Path...
All You Have To Lose Is Fear

Your way is yours. Each person's is different and all are valid.

Here we are at Chapter 16 and we're still getting started. Spiritual growth is never finished. We can deny, disguise and fool ourselves, but beneath it all, we know the Creator sees us in truth.

Using the steps described in this guidebook, you can treat yourself and your life with compassion, commitment, willingness, patience and faith. You can find and heal your anger, judgment, fear and guilt. You can find teachers along the way and keep the channels open to Divine Guidance. You can locate and remove blocks by using all the tools and you can create inner peace for yourself. You will do this in a way that suits you and changes as you do.

Following your own path is living your own truth in the world — speaking your truth without backing down. It is being true to yourself moment to moment, in ways you never imagined possible. Being true to yourself means you accept that others in your world are your teachers, not your "trials," provocateurs or enemies. When you live your own truth, you accept that *you are the expert on you* and you act in alignment with that knowledge.

You may fear that you will lose precious friendships if you reveal too much about how you really feel, and you don't have the courage to act on those feelings. The reality is that if you live your truth you will lose only fear, not friendship. If people leave you because you don't have sex on a first date or because you wear a fur coat or you vote a different political party, they aren't genuine friends. Friends allow plenty of room for you to be who you really are. Be that kind of friend to yourself first and it will be easier to allow others to give such friendship to you.

Releasing Outmoded Beliefs And Behaviors

It is helpful to examine the ways you think and behave because as you learn more about what fits with living your own truth, you'll need to release some old, outdated behaviors and beliefs to make room for the ones that are more suited to you now.

Ask yourself about this behavior, for example. Do you find that you seek permission from others before you begin something new, such as buying a car or dating someone new? How often do your choices — whether big or small — reflect your efforts to please others? Being a people-pleaser indicates that you're not attuned to what your higher self wants. Even though you know that it's physically impossible to please everybody, you can get caught up in the effort out of fear.

Fear whispers the frightening "truth." You couldn't possibly know how to do it right; you must rely on outside direction or you will fail. If you fail, "they" won't like you. Or, fear warns, if you please yourself without considering others first, you're selfish. If you're selfish, you're not nice. And if you're not nice, people will abandon you. (Did you ever notice how many lose-lose situations the fear mind sets up?) Can you see how this old way of thinking keeps you from discovering what you are capable of? How will you ever know if you allow old fears to keep you from experimenting, taking risks, and living your truth in the world?

In the next exercise, see if you can identify some of the beliefs and behaviors that keep you from living your own truth. Explore each behavior (with compassion) by asking yourself:

    1) Who am I trying to please?

    2) How does it feel to me?

    3) What reason do I give myself for this attempt to please?

For example, suppose you check in with your mother by telephone once a day. You do it to please her, but you find yourself feeling tense. You feel like you really having nothing to say to her. But, you tell yourself, you have to show her you love her. You have to reassure her constantly. Is she feeling reassured? Is it ever enough? No.

EXERCISE 16-1

Who Are You Trying to Please?

Use a page in your journal to make four columns as below. List as many situations as you can think of in column A and then use the remaining columns to help you think about how this behavior works for you.

    A. Who are you trying to please?

    B. How does it feel?

    C. What is your reason for trying to please?

    D. Is it working?

Becoming conscious of this kind of limiting behavior is a necessary step in self-knowledge. Until you know yourself, you can not be true to yourself. Becoming conscious opens the door to growth, both on a personal and a soul level. Please step lightly into this new self-awareness. Be compassionate with yourself. Self-judgment only slows you down. Your work here is gathering information about yourself, not finding and punishing flaws. If letting go of old behaviors and beliefs is difficult or inconceivable, know that fear is the glue keeping you stuck.

Current behaviors are choices, even though they may be choices beyond your awareness. ☺ *You can always make new conscious choices once you identify and release old ones.*

You have an unlimited number of choices available to you.
You have an unlimited amount of time in which to do your spiritual work.

The concept of infinite choice and infinite time causes great discomfort in people who firmly believe in goals, structure or control. Oddly enough, though, preoccupation with deadlines and limits can frighten you into inaction. Consider the terror that can be generated by the following statements that run through so many people's minds:

◊ Do it right the first time

◊ There are no second chances

◊ I need more (and more) information before I can act

◊ Wait until someone tells you the time is right

When you move toward your own awakening into consciousness, you move toward freeing yourself from the control of:

◊ Limiting messages from your fearful mind

◊ Running your life on "automatic pilot"

◊ Pleasing everyone else before (or instead of) pleasing yourself

◊ The cultural trance (the way "we" do things)

As you find your own path and honor the beliefs and behaviors you need to embrace to stay true to yourself, your more aware self will take over. This new-found self guides with love and compassion rather than prodding with fear and harsh self-judgment. The different approach will feel foreign to you initially. You will notice that the clamor in your head has diminished; that you are experiencing entire moments of inner peace.

People at this stage often are confused by this shift in consciousness. They think they're "losing it" because they forget many of the items on their "to do" lists, they've lost their sense of ambition and they yearn to sit in sunbeams! I always reassure people at this stage. I remind them that God gave us sunbeams to sit in. (Cats have known this for millennia.) This transition is part of the process of spiritual growth. After awhile they will settle into this new relaxed way of being. Once they have reached this state, many people can no longer imagine driving themselves as hard as they once did. They recognize that life has a flow and that each person operates her own floodgates.

When you are living in tune with your higher nature, with your truth, you are quietly listening rather than performing. You are enough without having to prove it to yourself constantly. When the critical mind chimes in and decries your lack of activity, your lack of productivity, it is actually encouraging you to go unconscious again. ☯ *Remaining conscious or returning to remote control is a moment-by-moment choice for you.* Once you see it as choice, you can decide as needed, without self-judgment. If a choice you make seems out of line with who you are, choose again. When you spend time regretting your choices or blaming yourself for mistakes, you waste time (and that is also a choice).

EXERCISE 16-2

How Are You Holding Yourself Captive?

Finding old beliefs and automatic responses is liberating. Once the clutter is cleared away, you can begin to discover your truth. Think about your current situation and changes that have been just on the outer edge of your vision. To bring them into clearer focus, write down what your old response has been and how you imagine it could be different. For example, if fear of the unknown has kept you in a dead-end job, you may have been toying with the idea of updating your resume and sending it out. Once you define the desired change, you are more clear about whether it feels right for you and what's been blocking your way. For each situation you list, consider the old choice and the desired change.

Everything is spiritual when seen through the eyes of the heart.

Even though the mind labels things good or bad, spiritual or not spiritual, the mind simply cannot comprehend the limitless universe, The way. ☺ *The only true interpreter of spiritual life is your compassionate heart.* It is the only valid choice-maker. Realizing this truth is a big step on your path. Once you embrace this position consciously, you may never again view life the same way. You will certainly more quickly notice old ways of thinking. When you make a choice out of fear, you only generate more fear. God doesn't judge you for which choice you make. Can you imagine a life where you feel free to make your own choices and live as your inner self directs you? What fears does that bring up?

How do you make the switch from fear to truth? One thought at a time. Yes, it's that simple. And that difficult! One way is to listen to your body. Your body will call for your attention with headaches, knots in the stomach, shaky hands, teary eyes, etc. When you pay attention to what your body is telling you, you can use physical responses to lead you home to your true self. When you have a physical response, you're having an emotional response. Breathe into your physical sensation. It will tell you what the emotion is and how strong it is. When you breathe into a feeling, it will appear to intensify, but in reality it is just opening so that you can transform it. Locate it, breathe into it and experience it, and then it transforms. As you locate and heal each damaged cell of your spiritual self, you free up more of your energy to be who you really are.

The goal of spiritual growth is to
become conscious, not to force perfection.

Your life is offering you information about your old beliefs. Until you know what you have been believing until now, you will be unable to recognize new choices. Becoming aware of choices is the elegant dance of a soul owning a life. Forward step, you make a choice. Side step, you feel unsure of your choice and consider others. A twirl, you review past choices in the hope of making more sure-footed choices in the future. Be sure to listen for self-judgments along the way and disconnect them. They are rote material drawn from the past. They have no relevance beyond your being aware that some are still there. Removing self-judgments from your path unblocks your progress.

As you become more aware of the part you play in creating many of the difficulties in your life, you will begin to recognize alternative choices for yourself. If you've always done something in a certain way, or always reacted a certain way, consider your part in that. What are your fundamental beliefs about relationships or food or family? Are your beliefs creating your reactions? If so, are you willing to stop and take a look at your old beliefs with an eye to releasing them to make room for beliefs that are your truth rather than something you were taught as a child? With your new choices, you will be acting from your own center rather than from borrowed beliefs. You will be creating a living belief system.

Once you begin choosing, more choices will present themselves. The universe is very generous with the number of choices it offers! There is truly a river of choice and it is dammed only by fear. Until you remove the dam of fear, that river is prevented from flowing. But it's out there waiting.

*You don't have to create the choices, you
only have to remove the blockage and let the choices flow to you.*

If you cannot see the dam in your river of choices, you can ask yourself:

How am I getting in the way of all my soul wants for me?

Or, when you are ready, you can affirm to yourself:

I am willing to let go of the ways in which I block my good.

Until you begin to shed light on the darkness of fear, it will remain in power, able to confuse you and assert control. Taking responsibility for your own awareness is the first step in the process of self-development. It calls for careful attunement to the heart's knowing. Using your new living belief system, unlike your former rigid and unquestioned system, you will continually make choices, weaving in or eliminating strands in the fabric of your soul, refining it and becoming more balanced and peaceful.

You have chosen to walk consciously on your spiritual path, to develop and refine yourself for the growth of your soul and the glory of God. Do it. One thought at a time. Be in each moment as much as you possibly can.

EXERCISE 16-3

Ask yourself:

As you have seen throughout this book, clarifying and quantifying who you are and what you're doing enables you to grow. Clearing out the old makes room for the new. When given deep consideration, the questions below will help you focus on where you are on your spiritual journey. Answer them again and again as you move forward. Notice your growth — it's your reward!

- *What do I see?*

- *What do I know to be true?*

- *How do I express my truth?*

- *What purpose does what's happening in this moment serve in my life? Use your journal!*

If you came to this book seeking easy answers, you have found them. If you read through these pages to find suffering and struggle, you have also found that. You create your experiences and your reality in order to develop your soul. Let that be the first awareness you have, and the one you come to in order to center yourself whenever you need to.

I hope you will return to this book again and again as you make your journey. You will find its meaning fuller after each year of living, experiencing and growing. You can use it to steer your path closer to The way. Or to gain understanding of the process. Or to remind yourself of who you are and what you know. There will be more life, more experiences, more teachers and more lessons. That is the journey all souls must make. That is The way. The way is. It is sent with love.

Chapter 16
Tools For Following your own path

    ☘   You can make new conscious choices once you identify and release unconscious old ones.

    ☘   Remaining conscious or returning to remote control is a moment-to-moment choice.

    ☘   The only true interpreter of spiritual life is your compassionate heart.

Index

Index

Order Form

To order this book directly from Rosalind Thompson, please send your check or money order to:

Rosalind Thompson
P.O. Box 71
El Granada, CA 94018

Please send _____ copies of *Paths Are Made by Walking*

$18.95 each: _____

Shipping & Handling: $2.00 per book: _____

8.25% Sales Tax (California addresses only): _____

Total Amount Enclosed: _____

Autographed to: _____

Name _____

Address _____

City _____

State _____ Zip Code _____